Table of Contents

D1594916

Practice Test #1

Practice Questions

1. A registered principal or registered representative must retake the qualifying exam if his or her registration has been revoked or terminated for a period of _____ or more.
   a. 1 year
   b. 2 years
   c. 3 years
   d. 5 years

2. A member may maintain a representative registration for which of the following persons?
   I.   A person who performs legal, compliance, or internal audit functions for the member
   II. A person who performs back-office functions for the member
   III. A person who is no longer functioning as a representative
   IV. A person who performs administrative functions for registered personnel

   a. I & II only
   b. I, II, III
   c. I, II & IV
   d. I, II, III, IV

3. Which of the following is true regarding persons who are to function as research analysts?
   a. They must pass a qualifying examination for research analysts only.
   b. They must be registered as a general securities representative only.
   c. They must be registered as a general securities representative and pass a qualifying examination for research analysts.
   d. None of the above.

4. Within how many days must a member report to FINRA if the member or an associated person of the member is the subject of a written customer complaint involving allegations of theft or misappropriation of funds?
   a. 10 business days
   b. 15 calendar days
   c. 20 business days
   d. 30 calendar days

5. Which of the following are considered institutional investors?
   a. A governmental entity
   b. An employee benefit plan that meets the requirement of Section 403(b) or Section 457 of the Internal Revenue Code and has at least 100 participants
   c. A qualified plan as defined in Section 3(a)(12)(C) of the Exchange Act and that has at least 100 participants
   d. All of the above

6. An options contract that gives the holder the right to purchase the number of shares of the underlying security is a _____.
   a. Put
   b. Covered
   c. Uncovered
   d. Call

7. Which of the following registered principals may approve the purchase of a variable annuity?
   I.   General Securities Sales Supervisor (Series 9/10)
   II.   General Securities Principal (Series 24)
   III. Investment Company Products/Variable Contracts Principal (Series 26)

   a. I only
   b. III only
   c. I & III
   d. I, II, & III

8. Correspondence means any written communication that is distributed to ____ or fewer retail investors within any _____-day period.
   a. 10 or fewer investors within any 10-day period
   b. 15 or fewer investors within any 20-day period
   c. 25 or fewer investors within any 30-day period
   d. 30 or fewer investors within any 25-day period

9. According to NASD Rule 2711 a research analyst's report may be reviewed by non-research personnel for which of the following reasons?
   a. to ensure that there is no slanderous information about them in the report
   b. to see if the information has been used in a previous report
   c. to see if they agree with the report or not
   d. to ensure the factual accuracy of the report

10. What is the Time of Day Restriction when placing cold calls (telemarketing)?
   a. Before 8:00 a.m. and after 9:00 p.m. (local time of the caller's location)
   b. Before 8:00 a.m. and after 9:00 p.m. (local time of the called party's location)
   c. Before 8:00 a.m. and after 8:00 p.m. (local time of the caller's location)
   d. Before 8:00 a.m. and after 8:00 p.m. (local time of the called party's location)

11. What are the three General Telemarketing Requirements?
   a. Time of Day Restriction, State Do-Not-Call List, and National Do-Not-Call List
   b. State Do-Not-Call List, National Do-Not-Call List, and Firm-Specific Do-Not-Call List
   c. Time of Day Restriction, Firm-Specific Do-Not-Call List, and State Do-Not Call List
   d. Time of Day Restriction, National Do-Not-Call List, and Firm-Specific Do Not Call List

12. What is the dollar value that any gift from or to a member or person associated with a member may not exceed in one year?
   a. $0.00 (gifts are not allowed)
   b. $50.00
   c. $100.00
   d. $150.00

13. When must a customer opening a margin account receive the Margin Disclosure Statement?
   a. After the account is opened
   b. At or prior to account opening
   c. With the first account statement
   d. When the first deposit into the account is made

14. Which of the following is not a disclosure in the Margin Disclosure Statement?
   a. You can lose more funds than you deposit in the margin account.
   b. The firm can sell your securities or other assets without contacting you.
   c. You can make bigger profits by utilizing margin in your account.
   d. You are not entitled to choose which securities or other assets in your account(s) are liquidated or sold to meet a margin call.

15. How often must the Margin Disclosure Statement be sent to existing margin account holders?
   a. Monthly
   b. Quarterly
   c. Semiannually
   d. Annually

16. Which of the following statements are true regarding FINRA's margin maintenance requirements?
   I.   25 percent of the current market value of all margin securities
   II. $2.50 per share or 100 percent of the current market value, whichever is greater, of each stock "short" in the account selling at less than $5.00 per share
   III. $5.00 per share or 30 percent of the current market value, whichever is greater, of each stock "short" in the account selling at $5.00 per share or above
   IV.   5 percent of the principal amount or 30 percent of the current market value, whichever is greater, of bonds "short" in the account
   V.   100 percent of the current market value for each non-margin eligible equity security held "long" in the account

   a. I, II, III
   b. I, II, IV
   c. I, III, V
   d. I, II, III, IV, V

17. If a client purchases 500 shares of ABC Corp. at $10.00 per share, what is the initial margin requirement if the house maintenance requirement is 30 percent?
   a. $1.250.00
   b. $1,500.00
   c. $2,500.00
   d. $5,000.00

18. Which of the following would be considered a "Breakpoint Sale"?
   a. A customer purchasing $150,000 in multiple mutual funds and paying the full sales charge of each.
   b. A customer receiving a 20 percent discount on an equity trade.
   c. A customer purchasing a municipal bond above par.
   d. A customer purchasing a corporate bond below par.

19. Excessive trading in a customer's account for no apparent reason other than to generate commissions is _____.
   a. Churning
   b. Rebalancing
   c. Market timing
   d. Front running

20. A registered representative trading an equity based on non-public information in his or her own account before trading for clients is called _____.
   a. Churning
   b. Rebalancing
   c. Market timing
   d. Front running

21. Which of the following are prohibited activities?
   a. Churning
   b. Front running
   c. Insider trading
   d. All of the above

22. Which of the following is not a prohibited activity?
   a. Rebalancing
   b. Commingling funds
   c. Guarantees against loss
   d. Spreading market rumors

23. Which of the following items regarding SIPC must member firms advise all new customers of in writing when opening a new account?
   I.   The SIPC website address
   II.   The SIPC telephone number
   III.   How to obtain the SIPC brochure

   a. I only
   b. I and III
   c. I and II
   d. I, II, and III

24. When using a hypothetical illustration to compare a variable life insurance policy to a term policy, what is the greatest rate of return that may be used?
   a. 8 percent
   b. 10 percent
   c. 12 percent
   d. 14 percent

25. Which of the following is not a general consideration regarding communications with the public about variable life insurance and variable annuities?
   a. Prospectus delivery
   b. Product Identification
   c. Liquidity
   d. Claims about guarantees

- 4 -

26. Any material for use in any newspaper, magazine, or other public medium, or by radio, television, or telephone recording, is referred to as _____.
   a. An advertisement
   b. A market letter
   c. A research report
   d. Sales literature

27. Which of the following terms refers to printed or processed analysis covering individual companies or industries?
   a. Advertisement
   b. Market letter
   c. Research report
   d. Sales literature

28. Which of the following is true regarding recommendations?
   a. Must have a reasonable basis
   b. The market price at the time of the recommendation must be shown
   c. Supporting information should be provided or offered
   d. All of the above

29. What is the minimum time period that may be used in material promoting past records of research recommendations in connection with purchases or sales?
   a. Six months
   b. One year
   c. Three years
   d. Five years

30. When using testimonials, which of the following points does not need to be clearly stated in the body copy of the material?
   a. The testimonial may not be representative of the experience of other clients.
   b. The fact that that it is a paid testimonial if a nominal sum is paid.
   c. If the testimonial concerns a technical aspect of investing, the person making the testimonial must have adequate knowledge and experience to form a valid opinion.
   d. The testimonial cannot be indicative of future performance or success.

31. How often must registered representatives complete FINRA's Regulatory Element continuing education program?
   a. Every year
   b. Every two years
   c. Every three years
   d. Every five years

32. When must a U-5 be filed?
   a. At the time of employment with a member firm
   b. At the time of termination of employment from a member firm
   c. Annually for each registered representative employed by a member firm
   d. Every three years for each registered representative employed by a member firm

33. Annual continuing education training provided by member firms is known as_____.
    a. Firm Continuing Education
    b. Compliance Training
    c. Firm Element Training
    d. Firm Regulatory Training

34. Registered Investment Advisers are registered through the _____.
    a. FINRA
    b. SEC
    c. MSRB
    d. NYSE

35. When must political contributions be disclosed to the MSRB?
    a. Quarterly
    b. Semiannually
    c. Annually
    d. Never

36. Which of the following items does not need to be reported on a U-4?
    a. Bankruptcy
    b. DUI
    c. Medical condition
    d. Address change

37. Which of the following is not a requirement for advertisements of investment company products that utilize rankings?
    a. The name of the category (i.e., high yield)
    b. The name of the ranking entity
    c. Past performance is indicative of future results
    d. The time period and its ending date

38. New-issue municipal securities advertisements have the additional requirements of which of the following:
     I.   Accuracy at time of sale
    II.   Source of data
   III.   Accuracy at time of publication
    IV.   Currentness of calculation

    a. I only
    b. II and III
    c. I and III
    d. IV only

39. Prior to the Options Disclosure Document (ODD) being delivered, a registered representative may do which of the following:
    a. Solicit a sale of an options contract as long as the ODD is sent before or at the time of sale
    b. Place an options trade for a client's account as long as the ODD is sent the same day
    c. Place an options trade for a client's account as long as the ODD is sent before settlement
    d. Limit discussions to general descriptions of the options

- 6 -

40. Which of the following is false regarding options-related advertisements?
    a. Must be approved in advance by a Registered Options Principal
    b. Copies must be retained by the member firm
    c. Records containing the name of the persons who created and approved the advertisement must be kept
    d. FINRA never needs to approve options-related advertisements

41. Which of the following statements are true with respect to options communications that include historical performance?
    a. A Registered Options Principal determines that the records or statistics fairly present the status of the recommendations or transactions reported upon
    b. All relevant costs, including commissions, fees, and daily margin obligations, are disclosed and reflected in the performance
    c. They must state that the results presented should not and cannot be viewed as an indicator of future performance
    d. All of the above

42. A municipal security advertisement that concerns the facilities, services, or skills with respect to municipal securities of such broker, dealer, or municipal securities dealer or of another broker, dealer, or municipal securities dealer is the definition of _____.
    a. Professional advertisement
    b. Product advertisement
    c. New issue product advertisement
    d. Municipal fund security product advertisement

43. Before a registered representative may recommend the purchase or exchange of a deferred variable annuity, he or she must have a reasonable basis to believe all of the following except:
    a. The transaction is suitable
    b. The customer will not need the funds invested
    c. The customer would benefit from certain features such as tax-deferred growth
    d. The customer has been informed of various features such as a surrender period and surrender charge

44. Which of the following is false regarding collateralized mortgage obligation (CMO) advertisements?
    a. Advertisements may not contain a comparison with any other investment vehicle.
    b. Advertisements may contain comparisons with CDs.
    c. Advertisements must include a description of the initial issue tranche.
    d. Advertisements that contain an anticipated yield must disclose the prepayment assumption used to calculate the yield.

45. A member may not publish a research report regarding a subject company for which the member acted as manager or co-manager of an IPO for _____ days following the date of the offering.
    a. 20 calendar days
    b. 20 business days
    c. 40 calendar days
    d. 40 business days

46. A member may not publish a research report regarding a subject company for which the member acted as manager or co-manager of a secondary offering for _____ days following the date of the offering.
   a. 10 calendar days
   b. 10 business days
   c. 20 calendar days
   d. 20 business days

47. Which of the following is true regarding price targets in research reports?
   a. The valuation method used to determine the price target must be disclosed.
   b. Price targets must have a reasonable basis.
   c. Price targets must be accompanied by a disclosure concerning the risks that may impede achievement of the price target.
   d. All of the above.

48. Which of the following items are required in a research report that contains ratings?
   a. The meaning of each rating must be defined.
   b. The percentage of all securities rated by the member to which the member would assign a "buy," "hold/neutral," or "sell" rating must be disclosed.
   c. The member must disclose the percentage of subject companies within the "buy," "hold/neutral," and "sell" ratings for whom the member has provided investment banking services within the previous 12 months.
   d. All of the above.

49. Which of the following is true regarding third-party research reports?
   a. A third-party research report is a research report produced by a person in the research department of a member firm.
   b. Third-party research reports and independent third-party research reports have the same meaning.
   c. A registered principal (or supervisory analyst) must approve all third-party research reports distributed by a member.
   d. A registered principal (or supervisory analyst) must approval all independent third-party research reports.

50. Which of the following must be disclosed in a research report?
   a. Ownership and material conflicts of interest
   b. Receipt of compensation
   c. If the member was making a market in the subject company's securities at the time that research report was published
   d. All of the above

51. Which of the following written communications is considered a research report?
   a. An email that includes an analysis of equity securities of individual companies
   b. A discussion of broad-based indices
   c. A commentary on economic, political, or market conditions
   d. A technical analysis concerning the demand and supply for a sector, index, or industry based on trading volume and price

52. Which of the following accounts is not covered by FDIC?
    a. Bank savings and checking accounts
    b. Mutual fund account
    c. Bank money market account
    d. Certificates of deposit

53. What is the tentative prospectus circulated by the underwriters of a new of stock that is pending approval the SEC?
    a. Red herring
    b. IPO
    c. Registration statement
    d. Private placement

54. What is the limit of SIPC protection if a brokerage firm fails?
    a. $100,000
    b. $250,000
    c. $500,000
    d. $1,000,000

55. What is the limit of FDIC protection per depositor, per insured bank, for each account ownership category?
    a. $100,000
    b. $250,000
    c. $500,000
    d. $1,000,000

56. Beginning in 2014, what is the basic exclusion limit on tax-free transfers during life or at death (the unification of gift and estate taxes)?
    a. $2,250,000
    b. $2,340,000
    c. $5,250,000
    d. $5,340,000

57. If a person has made lifetime gifts totaling $2,000,000 and dies in 2014, what is the amount that will be paid in taxes if the total remaining estate is $10,000,000?
    a. $1,864,000
    b. $2,664,000
    c. $3,200,000
    d. $4,000,000

58. What is the maximum amount that may be gifted within one calendar year to avoid taxation?
    a. $10,000
    b. $11,000
    c. $12,000
    d. $14,000

59. What is the cost basis of securities given as a gift?
   a. The average of the high and low prices on the date of the gift
   b. The purchase price of the securities when they were originally bought
   c. The average of the current market price and the price originally paid
   d. The average of the high and low prices on the date of the original purchase

60. What is the cost basis of securities received as an inheritance?
   a. The current market price at the time the securities are received by the heir
   b. The purchase price of the securities when they were originally bought
   c. The average of the high and the low prices on the date of death
   d. The average of the high and low prices on the date of the original purchase

61. A _____ refers to when a company first sells it shares to the public.
   a. Initial public offering
   b. Initial marketing
   c. Initial sales offering
   d. Initial rights offering

62. Which of the following are true regarding tombstone ads?
   I.   They present an offer to sell.
   II.   They must identify the issuer's name.
   III. They must include the name, address, and toll-free telephone number of the person or
         entity from whom a prospectus may be obtained.
   IV.   They must disclose the anticipated security rating.

   a. I, II
   b. II, III
   c. I, II, III
   d. I, II, III, IV

63. Which of the following is not a purpose of the Securities Act of 1933?
   a. Require that investors receive financial and other significant information
   b. Guarantee the financial information received by investors is accurate
   c. Prohibit deceit, misrepresentations, and fraud in the sale of securities
   d. Require the registration of securities

64. Which of the following securities are exempt from registration under the Securities Act of 1933?
   a. Common stock
   b. Municipal bond
   c. Corporate bond
   d. Preferred stock

65. The SEC was created under _____.
   a. The Securities Act of 1933
   b. The Securities Exchange Act of 1934
   c. Investment Company Act of 1940
   d. Investment Advisers Act of 1940

66. Which of the following is an SRO?
    a. New York Stock Exchange
    b. NASDAQ Stock Market
    c. Chicago Board of Options
    d. All of the above

67. _____ has the power to register, regulate, and oversee brokerage firms, transfer agents, and clearing agencies as well as SROs.
    a. NASD
    b. FINRA
    c. SEC
    d. MSRB

68. Which act created the "Public Company Accounting Oversight Board"?
    a. Dodd-Frank Wall Street Reform and Consumer Protection Act of 2010
    b. Sarbanes-Oxley Act of 2002
    c. Investment Advisers Act of 1940
    d. Trust Indenture Act of 1939

69. Which of the following financial information is not required on a new account application?
    a. Net worth
    b. Annual income
    c. Liabilities
    d. Liquid net worth

70. Which of the following items should not be taken into consideration when determining investment suitability?
    a. Annual income
    b. Investment experience
    c. Net worth
    d. None of the above

71. Which of the following item(s) can affect an investor's risk tolerance?
    a. Age
    b. Time frame
    c. Personal experience
    d. All of the above

72. The length of time an investor plans to keep an investment is known as the _____.
    a. Holding period
    b. Time horizon
    c. Quiet period
    d. Calendar period

73. Which of the following investments would be most appropriate for an investor with an objective of capital preservation?
    a. Preferred stock
    b. Certificate of deposit
    c. Municipal bond
    d. Corporate bond

74. Which of the following investments would not be considered appropriate for an investor with an objective of current income?
    a. Growth stock
    b. Municipal bond
    c. Corporate bond
    d. Utility stock

75. Which of the following investments would not be appropriate for an investor with a capital growth objective?
    a. Unit investment trust
    b. Common stock
    c. Growth mutual fund
    d. Zero coupon bond

76. What is another name for the investment objective of "total return"?
    a. Growth
    b. Income
    c. Growth and income
    d. Preservation of capital

77. What is the tax advantage of owning municipal bonds?
    a. No federal taxes
    b. No state taxes regardless of your state of residence
    c. No state taxes if the municipality is in your state of residence
    d. Both A and C

78. Investing in multiple investment vehicles within a portfolio to reduce risk or increase returns is called _____.
    a. Dollar cost averaging
    b. Discounting
    c. Diversification
    d. Distribution

79. Which of the following scenarios is the best example of diversification?
    a. An investor buys 1,000 shares of ABC stock at $25 per share
    b. An investor who invests $25,000 in one corporate bond
    c. An investor who invests $25,000 in a large cap growth mutual fund
    d. An investor who invests a total of $25,000 between stocks, bonds, and mutual funds.

80. _____ is the process of buying investment vehicles that have a high degree of uncertainty regarding their future value and expected earnings.
    a. Speculation
    b. Hedging
    c. Gambling
    d. Risk aversion

81. _____ risk refers to the impact that bad management decisions, other internal missteps, or external situations can have on a company's performance and on the value of investments in that company.
   a. Market
   b. Investment
   c. Financial
   d. Management

82. Which of the following statements is false regarding modern portfolio theory?
   a. It is a scientific approach to measuring risk.
   b. It guarantees against long-term losses.
   c. It involves calculating projected returns of various portfolio combinations.
   d. It is the concept of minimizing risk by combining volatile and price-stable investment in a single portfolio.

83. What is the beta of the market?
   a. -1.00
   b. 0.00
   c. 1.00
   d. None of the above

84. What is beta?
   a. A measure of risk
   b. A measure of value
   c. A measure of reward
   d. A measure of performance

85. Which of the following scenarios would be considered an unsuitable recommendation?
   a. Recommending a CD purchase to an elderly risk-averse investor
   b. Recommending a common stock to a 30-year-old with a growth objective
   c. Recommending a speculative stock to a recently retired investor who is risk averse
   d. Recommending a growth stock mutual fund to a 30-year-old investor with a growth objective

86. Which of the following is not a requirement for an investor to execute a short sale?
   a. The investor must own the stock being sold.
   b. The current inside bid must be higher than the previous inside bid.
   c. The seller must net all positions in the security.
   d. None of the above is a requirement for a short sale.

87. Under Regulation T, what is the maximum amount of the total purchase price of a stock for new purchases that a firm can lend a customer?
   a. 25 percent
   b. 50 percent
   c. 75 percent
   d. 100 percent

- 13 -

88. Which of the following are examples of information security to protect customers' personal information?
    a. Encrypted email
    b. Password-protected laptops
    c. Printing only the last four digits of Social Security numbers on documents
    d. All of the above

89. If a registered representative receives a customer complaint, what should he or she do first?
    a. Try to handle the customer by himself or herself
    b. Notify the branch manager or designated compliance individual
    c. Notify the Chief Compliance Officer of the broker-dealer
    d. Nothing

90. How often must firms notify employees of their business continuity or disaster recovery plans?
    a. Annually
    b. Semiannually
    c. Quarterly
    d. Monthly

91. Which of the following investments would be the least suitable for an elderly investor who is risk averse?
    a. Municipal bond
    b. Corporate bond
    c. Mutual fund
    d. Common stock

92. Which of the following investments would be most suitable for a young investor who can only invest a small amount each month?
    a. Common stock
    b. Corporate bond
    c. Options
    d. Mutual fund

93. Which of the following investments would be most suitable for an investor in a high tax bracket who wants to avoid paying any taxes on his investments?
    a. Corporate bond
    b. Municipal bond
    c. Mutual fund
    d. Preferred stock

94. Which of the following investors would be best suited to invest in U.S. Treasuries?
    a. A 25-year-old interested in speculative investments
    b. A 25-year-old with an investment objective of growth
    c. A retired individual with an investment objective of growth
    d. A retired individual with an investment objective of income

95. A corporate bond would be least suitable for which of the following investors?
    a. A 25-year-old interested in speculative investments
    b. A 25-year-old with an investment objective of growth and income
    c. A retired individual with an investment objective of growth and income
    d. A retired individual with an investment objective of income

96. What is margin in a brokerage account?
    a. The difference between the purchase price and the current value of each security.
    b. The difference between the beginning value and the current value of the entire account.
    c. Borrowed money that is used to purchase securities.
    d. Purchasing power in a cash account.

97. Under Regulation T, what are the initial and maintenance margin requirements?
    a. 25 percent initial / 25 percent maintenance
    b. 50 percent initial / 25 percent maintenance
    c. 50 percent initial / 30 percent maintenance
    d. 75 percent initial / 30 percent maintenance

98. In a joint tenancy with rights of survivorship (JTWROS) account, what happens to the assets when the first person dies?
    a. 50 percent of the assets are transferred to an estate account for the deceased person
    b. 100 percent of the assets remain with the surviving co-account holder
    c. 50 percent of the assets are transferred directly to the deceased person's heirs
    d. 100 percent of the assets are transferred to an estate account for the deceased person

99. In a community property state, how are assets divided between a husband and wife in a divorce?
    a. 100 percent belongs to the husband
    b. 100 percent belongs to the wife
    c. 50 percent belong to the husband and 50 percent belong to the wife
    d. 100 percent of the assets must remain jointly owned

100. At what age does a UTMA account terminate?
    a. 18
    b. 19
    c. 20
    d. 21

101. UTMA and UGMA accounts are registered under which person's Social Security number?
    a. The custodian
    b. The minor
    c. Either the custodian or the minor
    d. Neither the custodian nor the minor

102. Which of the following are advantages of a transfer on death (TOD) account?
    a. Avoids probate
    b. Assets pass directly to the beneficiaries
    c. Allows you to name beneficiaries on a taxable account
    d. All of the above

103. Who is/are the authorized person(s) on an estate account?
   a. An attorney
   b. A financial advisor
   c. The heir(s)
   d. The personal representative(s)

104. Which of the following documents may be used to give a third party trading authorization on an account?
   a. POA
   b. TOD
   c. Stock power
   d. Account agreement

105. _____ trading authority is when a person other than the account holder may invest without consulting the account holder about the price, amount, or type of security or the timing of the trades that are placed for the account.
   a. Discretionary
   b. Nondiscretionary
   c. Privileged
   d. Absolute

106. Which of the following is not a requirement for an employee of one broker-dealer opening an account with another broker-dealer?
   a. Duplicate brokerage account statements must be sent to the employee's broker-dealer upon request.
   b. Duplicate brokerage account confirms must be sent to the employee's broker-dealer upon request.
   c. The employee's broker-dealer must approve of the account before it is opened.
   d. Duplicate mutual fund company statements must be sent to the employee's broker-dealer.

107. How long must a member firm maintain client account statements?
   a. 1 year
   b. 3 years
   c. 6 years
   d. 10 years

108. How long must a member firm maintain client account confirms?
   a. 1 year
   b. 3 years
   c. 6 years
   d. 10 years

109. What transfer system do brokerage firms use to transfer accounts electronically?
   a. DRS
   b. DTC
   c. DWAC
   d. ACAT

110. If a client wishes to donate a stock to a charity that has a brokerage account at another firm, which system is most likely used to make the transfer?
    a. DRS
    b. DTC
    c. DWAC
    d. ACAT

111. Which of the following information is not required as part of the requirement to know your customer?
    a. Occupation and employer
    b. Investment experience
    c. Legal address
    d. Level of education

112. Which of the following would be a red flag when opening an account for a new client?
    a. No investment experience
    b. High annual income, but little or no savings
    c. Hesitant to give financial information
    d. Nervous or anxious when answering questions about objectives for the account

113. Which of the following account activities in a newly opened account would raise suspicions as a possible money laundering activity?
    a. Multiple deposits that are immediately wired out of the account to a foreign bank.
    b. Multiple deposits from other financial institutions that fund the purchases of several securities that remain in the account.
    c. One large deposit that is only partially invested in securities.
    d. Funds received via Fedwire

114. After what event was the USA PATRIOT Act created?
    a. The attack on the World Trade Center on September 11, 2001
    b. The attack on Pearl Harbor on December 7, 1941
    c. The bombing of the World Trade Center on February 26, 1993
    d. Boston Marathon terror attack on April 15, 2013

115. Which of the following would require a currency transaction report (CTR) to be filed?
    a. A single cash deposit of $15,000
    b. Two deposits of $5,000 made into the same bank account in one day
    c. Four deposits made at different bank branches totaling $12,000 into the same bank account on the same day
    d. All of the above

116. Designing a transaction to avoid triggering a reporting or recordkeeping requirement is called _____.
    a. Layering
    b. Fraud
    c. Structuring
    d. Laundering

117. _____ is the process that criminals use to try to hide or disguise the source of their illegal money by converting it into funds that appear legitimate.
    a. Layering
    b. Structuring
    c. Laundering
    d. Blackmail

118. All of the following are true regarding a suspicious activity report (SAR) except:
    a. The deadline to file a SAR is 30 calendar days after becoming aware of any suspicious transaction or pattern of suspicious transactions or activities.
    b. You are protected from civil liability when you report suspicious activity.
    c. You are only required to file a SAR if you believe the activity is suspicious and involves $2,000 or more.
    d. You must tell the person involved in the transaction that a SAR has been filed.

119. Which of the following persons are considered corporate insiders?
    a. Officers
    b. Directors
    c. Employees
    d. All of the above

120. The _____ of the U.S. Department of the Treasury administers and enforces economic and trade sanctions based on U.S. foreign policy and national security goals against targeted foreign countries and regimes.
    a. Import/Export Office
    b. Office of Foreign Assets Control
    c. Counter Terrorism Office
    d. Financial Crimes Network

121. The practice of buying and selling stocks rapidly throughout the day in the hope that the stocks will continue climbing or falling in value for the seconds to minutes that they are owned allowing for quick profits to be made is called _____.
    a. Buy and hold
    b. Active trading
    c. Market timing
    d. Day trading

122. A type of mutual fund or unit investment trust (UIT) whose investment objective is to achieve approximately the same return as a specific market index, such as the S&P 500, is called a(n) _____.
    a. Value fund
    b. Index fund
    c. Balanced fund
    d. Growth fund

123. Systematic risk is also known as _____.
    a. Market risk
    b. Credit risk
    c. Liquidity risk
    d. Interest rate risk

124. Which of the following investments would not be a suitable recommendation for an IRA?
    a. Common stock
    b. Corporate bond
    c. Municipal bond
    d. Mutual fund

125. Unsystematic risk is also known as _____.
    a. Market risk
    b. Purchasing power risk
    c. Credit risk
    d. Diversifiable risk

126. What type of risk involves the chance that Congress will make unfavorable changes in tax laws?
    a. Market risk
    b. Event risk
    c. Tax risk
    d. Liquidity risk

127. The possibility of higher prices in the future reducing the amount of goods or services that may be bought is known as _____.
    a. Market risk
    b. Purchasing power risk
    c. Financial risk
    d. Interest rate risk

128. The risk that a security will be redeemed prior to its maturity date is known as _____.
    a. Market risk
    b. Call risk
    c. Event risk
    d. Systematic risk

129. Which of the following terms is a maneuver used by a company that increases the number of shares outstanding by exchanging a specified number of new shares of stock for each outstanding share?
    a. Stock dividend
    b. Stock split
    c. Stock valuation
    d. Stock buyback

130. What is the statistic used to measure the dispersion around an asset's average or expected return, and the most common single indicator of an asset's risk?
    a. Alpha
    b. Beta
    c. Standard deviation
    d. Sharpe ratio

131. What is the name for stocks that have been sold and then repurchased (and held) by the issuing firm?
    a. Outstanding stock
    b. Treasury stock
    c. Issued stock
    d. Restricted stock

132. What type of bonds are high-risk securities that have received low ratings and produce high yields?
    a. Junk bonds
    b. Municipal bonds
    c. Junior bonds
    d. Preferred bonds

133. Investing a fixed dollar amount in a security at fixed intervals is known as _____.
    a. Asset allocation
    b. Diversification
    c. Budgeting
    d. Dollar cost averaging

134. _____ is an equity investment representing ownership in a corporation.
    a. Corporate bond
    b. Common stock
    c. Warrant
    d. Right

135. What is another name for an unrealized gain?
    a. Paper profit
    b. Capital gain
    c. Capital loss
    d. Hypothetical gain

136. What is the name of the strategy where a company reduces the number of shares outstanding by exchanging a fractional amount of a new share for each outstanding share of stock?
    a. Stock dividend
    b. Stock split
    c. Reverse stock split
    d. Reverse stock dividend

137. A company declares a 2:1 stock split. An investor who currently owns 100 shares of stock will have how many shares after the split?
    a. 50 shares
    b. 100 shares
    c. 150 shares
    d. 200 shares

138. If a company declares a 3:2 stock split, how many additional shares will an investor with 200 shares receive?
    a. 100 shares
    b. 200 shares
    c. 400 shares
    d. 600 shares

139. If a company declares a 1:2 reverse stock split, how many shares will an investor with 200 shares own after the split?
    a. 100 shares
    b. 200 shares
    c. 300 shares
    d. 400 shares

140. Selling a security to generate a loss and then immediately buying the security back is a _____.
    a. Capital loss
    b. Whipsaw
    c. Wash sale
    d. Tax loss sale

141. When interest rates increase, what happens to bond prices?
    a. Bond prices increase
    b. Bond prices decrease
    c. Bond prices may increase or decrease
    d. Changes in interest rate have no effect on bond prices

142. _____ is an intangible asset that is the result of the acquisition of one company by another for a premium value.
    a. Target value
    b. Book value
    c. Acquisition value
    d. Goodwill

143. What is an option for a long period of time to buy one or more shares of common stock in a given company at a price initially above the market price?
    a. Right
    b. Warrant
    c. Call
    d. Put

144. An option to buy shares of a new issue of common stock at a specified price, over a specified, fairly short period of time, is a _____.
    a. Right
    b. Warrant
    c. Call
    d. Put

145. Which of the following characteristics are true of preferred stocks?
   I.   Have a prior claim on the income and assets of the issuing firm
   II.   Have fixed dividends
   III. Issued as an alternative to debt
   IV.   Have an effect on EPS

   a. I and II
   b. I and III
   c. I, II, III
   d. I, II, III, IV

146. The market in which securities are traded after they have been issued is the _____?
   a. Primary market
   b. Money market
   c. Super market
   d. Secondary market

147. Which of the following statements is false regarding short selling?
   a. Money is made when prices fall.
   b. Short selling carries high risk and a limited return.
   c. Short selling carries low risk and an unlimited return.
   d. Money is lost when prices rise.

148. Dollar-denominated negotiable receipts for company stock of a foreign company held in trust in a foreign branch of a U.S. bank are _____.
   a. IPOs
   b. ADRs
   c. AMTs
   d. ATMs

149. Which of the following risks are associated with investing internationally?
   a. Foreign currency risk
   b. Market risk
   c. Event risk
   d. All of the above

Use the following information to answer the next three questions.
   ABC Corporation declared a $0.25 dividend to shareholders of record on Monday, December 5, payable on December 15. The closing price of ABC Corporation stock on December 5 is $20.34.

150. What is the dividend amount that a shareholder who owns 100 shares will receive?
   a. $0.25
   b. $2.50
   c. $25.00
   d. $250.00

151. What will the opening price of ABC Corporation be on December 6?
    a. $25.34
    b. $25.09
    c. $25.59
    d. Not enough information given

152. What is the last date that ABC Corporation stock can be purchased to receive the dividend?
    a. November 30
    b. December 5
    c. December 12
    d. December 15

153. How many stocks make up the Dow Jones Industrial Average (DJIA)?
    a. 25
    b. 30
    c. 100
    d. 500

154. Which of the following represents high-quality industrial stocks whose activities are believed to reflect overall market activity?
    a. Nasdaq Composite
    b. S&P 500
    c. DJIA
    d. Wilshire 5000

155. Which of the following types of stocks are considered defensive stocks?
    a. Public utilities
    b. Gold mining
    c. Technology companies
    d. Both A and B

156. You own 200 shares of XYZ Company that is currently trading at $25/share and will be receiving a 20 percent stock dividend. What will you receive on the payment date?
    a. $1,000
    b. $100
    c. 20 shares of XYZ stock
    d. 40 shares of XYZ stock

157. A customer purchases 100 shares of ABC stock at $35/share and pays $85 in commissions. What is the cost basis?
    a. $3,415
    b. $3,500
    c. $3,585
    d. $3,600

158. What is the maximum taxable rate on a long-term capital gain if you are in the highest income tax bracket?
    a. 10 percent
    b. 15 percent
    c. 20 percent
    d. 25 percent

159. How long must you hold an investment for it to be considered long term?
    a. 6 months
    b. 1 year
    c. 1 year and 1 day
    d. 2 years

160. _____ represents the resources of a company.
    a. Assets
    b. Liabilities
    c. Equity
    d. Cash flow

161. _____ represents the debts of a company.
    a. Assets
    b. Liabilities
    c. Equity
    d. Cash flow

162. What represents the amount of stockholders' capital in a firm?
    a. Assets
    b. Liabilities
    c. Equity
    d. Cash flow

163. Which financial statement shows the company's assets, liabilities, and shareholders' equity?
    a. Income statement
    b. Balance sheet
    c. Cash flow statement
    d. Annual report

164. Which financial statement provides a financial summary of the operating results of the company?
    a. Income statement
    b. Balance sheet
    c. Cash flow statement
    d. Annual report

165. Which financial statement provides a summary of the firm's cash flow and other events that caused changes in the cash position?
    a. Income statement
    b. Balance sheet
    c. Cash Flow statement
    d. Annual report

166. Municipal bonds backed by the full faith and credit, and taxing power, of the issuer are called
_____.
    a. Revenue bonds
    b. General obligation bonds
    c. Agency bonds
    d. Treasury notes

167. _____ are municipal bonds backed by the revenue-generating capacity of the issuer.
    a. Revenue bonds
    b. General obligation bonds
    c. Agency bonds
    d. Treasury notes

168. What is the graph called that represents the relationship between a bond's term to maturity and its yield at a given point in time?
    a. Efficient frontier
    b. Point and figure chart
    c. Yield curve
    d. Bar chart

169. Which of the following statements is false regarding an upward-sloping yield curve?
    a. It indicates that yields tend to increase with longer maturities.
    b. The longer the time span until maturity, the greater potential for price volatility.
    c. The longer the time span until maturity, the greater the risk for loss.
    d. It indicates that short-term rates are higher than long-term rates.

170. Which of the following statements is true regarding a downward-sloping yield curve?
    a. It indicates that yields tend to increase with longer maturities.
    b. It indicates that rates for short- and long-term loans are essentially the same.
    c. It indicates that intermediate term rates are the highest.
    d. It indicates that short-term rates are higher than long-term rates.

171. Which of the following mutual funds would be most likely to be passively managed?
    a. Bond fund
    b. Growth fund
    c. Income fund
    d. Index fund

172. What is the measure of bond price volatility that captures both price and reinvestment risks indicating how a bond will react to different interest rate environments?
    a. Yield
    b. Duration
    c. Immunization
    d. Beta

173. If interest rates are expected to rise in the near future, which of the following statements is true regarding duration?
   a. A longer duration would be preferred.
   b. A shorter duration would be preferred.
   c. There would be no preference regarding duration.
   d. A mid-term duration would be preferred.

174. An account in which customers with large portfolios pay a brokerage firm a flat annual fee that covers the cost of a money manager's services and the cost of commissions is called a _____ account.
   a. Cash
   b. Margin
   c. Collateral
   d. Wrap

Use the following information to answer the next six questions.

Net profit after taxes:	$18,000	Stockholder's Equity:	$170,000
Total revenues:	$615,000	Preferred dividends:	$5,000
Total assets:	$340,000	Number of common shares outstanding:	3,800
Current assets:	$280,000	Current liabilities:	$85,000
Earnings per share:	$4.75	Market price:	$49.50

175. What is the return on assets (ROA)?
   a. 2.92 percent
   b. 3.29 percent
   c. 4.76 percent
   d. 5.29 percent

176. What is the net profit margin?
   a. 10.59 percent
   b. 10.42 percent
   c. 2.92 percent
   d. 3.29 percent

177. What is the current ratio?
   a. 2.92 percent
   b. 3.29 percent
   c. 5.29 percent
   d. 10.59 percent

178. What is the return on equity (ROE)?
   a. 2.92 percent
   b. 10.59 percent
   c. 5.29 percent
   d. 10.42 percent

179. What is the P/E ratio?
    a. 10.42 percent
    b. 10.59 percent
    c. 5.29 percent
    d. 3.29 percent

180. What is the book value per share?
    a. $10.42
    b. $29.58
    c. $44.74
    d. $46.10

181. What is the term for the standard of conduct or moral judgment?
    a. Values
    b. Ethics
    c. Conscience
    d. Golden rule

182. What rating must a bond receive to be considered investment grade?
    a. Aaa/AAA
    b. Aa/AA
    c. A/A
    d. Baa/BBB

183. Calculating cost basis by selling the first shares that were bought is called _____.
    a. FIFO
    b. LIFO
    c. Average cost
    d. Estimating

184. Calculating cost basis by selling the most recent shares purchased is called _____.
    a. FIFO
    b. LIFO
    c. Average cost
    d. Estimating

185. Which of the following is not considered an organized securities market?
    a. NYSE
    b. NASDAQ
    c. CBOE
    d. CBT

186. Which of the following is the over-the-counter market?
    a. NYSE
    b. NASDAQ
    c. CBOE
    d. CBT

187. Which of the following statements is false regarding chart formations and technical analysis?
    a. Chart formations include head-and-shoulders, diamond, and triple top.
    b. Chartists believe the future course of the market is revealed in chart formations.
    c. Chartists believe the future course of the market cannot be determined.
    d. Chart formations give a buy or sell signal when the formation is broken.

188. What is the theory that the market price of securities always fully reflects available information making it difficult, if not impossible, to consistently outperform the market by picking "undervalued" stocks?
    a. Efficient frontier
    b. Efficient markets
    c. Random walk hypothesis
    d. Technical analysis

189. Which of the following statements best describes an income stock?
    a. Stocks that are unsurpassed in quality and have a long and stable record of earnings and dividends.
    b. Shares that have experienced, and are expected to continue experiencing, consistently high rates of growth in operations and earnings.
    c. Stocks that have a long and sustained record of paying higher-than-average dividends.
    d. Stocks of companies whose earnings are closely linked to the general level of business activity.

190. Which of the following statements best describes a blue chip stock?
    a. Stocks that are unsurpassed in quality and have a long and stable record of earnings and dividends.
    b. Shares that have experienced, and are expected to continue experiencing, consistently high rates of growth in operations and earnings.
    c. Stocks that have a long and sustained record of paying higher-than-average dividends.
    d. Stocks of companies whose earnings are closely linked to the general level of business activity.

191. Which of the following statements best describes a cyclical stock?
    a. Stocks that are unsurpassed in quality and have a long and stable record of earnings and dividends.
    b. Shares that have experienced, and are expected to continue experiencing, consistently high rates of growth in operations and earnings.
    c. Stocks that have a long and sustained record of paying higher-than-average dividends.
    d. Stocks of companies whose earnings are closely linked to the general level of business activity.

192. Which of the following statements best describes a growth stock?
    a. Stocks that are unsurpassed in quality and have a long and stable record of earnings and dividends.
    b. Shares that have experienced, and are expected to continue experiencing, consistently high rates of growth in operations and earnings.
    c. Stocks that have a long and sustained record of paying higher-than-average dividends.
    d. Stocks of companies whose earnings are closely linked to the general level of business activity.

193. An order to buy or sell a stock at the best available price when the order is placed is a _____ order.
   a. Limit
   b. Stop
   c. Market
   d. Stop limit

194. An order to buy a stock at specific price or better is what type of order?
   a. Limit order
   b. Stop order
   c. Market order
   d. Stop limit order

195. Which of the following is an example of a limit order?
   a. An order to sell 100 shares of XYZ at the best price available
   b. An order to sell 100 shares of XYZ (currently trading at $50) if the price drops to $45
   c. An order to buy 100 shares of XYZ at the best price available
   d. An order to buy 100 shares of XYZ at $40 or less

196. Which of the following is an example of a stop order?
   a. An order to sell 100 shares of XYZ at the best price available
   b. An order to sell 100 shares of XYZ (currently trading at $50) if the price drops to $45
   c. An order to buy 100 shares of XYZ at the best price available
   d. An order to buy 100 shares of XYZ at $40 or less

197. A stop limit order to sell 100 shares of ABC Corporation (ABC) stock at $35 is entered when the current market price of ABC stock is $45. The company announces lower-than-expected earnings and the stock price falls dramatically. Under which of the following scenarios will the order not execute?
   a. The market price immediately falls to $35 and then rebounds to trade between $35 and $36 before falling below $35 again.
   b. The market price immediately falls to $35 and continues to fall without rebounding.
   c. The market price immediately falls to $35 and continues to trade between $33 and $36.
   d. The market price immediately falls to $35 and continues to trade between $35 and $37.

198. Which of the following is not required on an order ticket?
   a. Customer name
   b. Account number
   c. Order type
   d. Symbol

199. A letter of intent allows an investor to purchase shares of a mutual fund at a reduced sales charge as long as the investor purchases the total amount necessary within what time period?
   a. 12 months
   b. 13 months
   c. 15 months
   d. 18 months

200. It is the responsibility of the _____ to ensure that a customer receives the correct breakpoint.
    a. Registered representative
    b. Customer
    c. Mutual fund company
    d. Broker-dealer

201. How often must customers receive account statements from an investment company?
    a. Monthly
    b. Quarterly
    c. Semiannually
    d. Annually

202. How often must customers receive account statements from a brokerage firm?
    a. Monthly, regardless of activity
    b. Monthly, if activity, otherwise semiannually
    c. Monthly, if activity, otherwise quarterly
    d. Quarterly, regardless of activity

203. A stock trade executed on Friday, January 2, will settle on what date?
    a. Monday, January 5
    b. Tuesday, January 6
    c. Wednesday, January 7
    d. Thursday, January 8

204. A stock trade executed on Wednesday, December 31, will settle on what date?
    a. Monday, January 5
    b. Tuesday, January 6
    c. Wednesday, January 7
    d. Thursday, January 8

205. If an option expires without hitting its strike price, what happens to the buyer and seller?
    a. The seller keeps the premium received and the buyer loses the premium paid.
    b. The seller keeps the premium received and loses the shares of the underlying security.
    c. The buyer loses the premium paid, but receives the shares of the underlying security.
    d. Nothing happens.

Use the following information to answer the next 5 questions:
    ABC   L 54.65 CHG -1.11 B 54.64 A 54.67 VLM 180758
    ABC CORP   AH 65.15 AL 48.34 YLD 0.00

206. What is the bid?
    a. 54.65
    b. 54.64
    c. 54.67
    d. 65.15

207. What is the ask?
    a. 54.65
    b. 54.64
    c. 54.67
    d. 65.15

208. What was the price of the last trade?
    a. 54.65
    b. 54.64
    c. 54.67
    d. 65.15

209. Does ABC stock currently pay a dividend?
    a. Yes
    b. No
    c. Not enough information given
    d. None of the above

210. What is the spread?
    a. $0.01
    b. $0.02
    c. $0.03
    d. $0.04

211. During the course of a trading day, when a stock's price goes up, it is known as _____.
    a. An increase
    b. An uptick
    c. A downtick
    d. A gain

212. What is the difference between NAV and POP?
    a. NAV is the actual price of a mutual fund share while POP is the NAV plus a sales charge.
    b. NAV is the net asset value of the mutual fund and POP is the public offering price.
    c. Both A and B
    d. None of the above

213. Which of the following investors may purchase shares of a mutual fund at NAV?
    a. Employees of the mutual fund company
    b. A registered representative
    c. Investors purchasing shares inside a wrap account
    d. All of the above

214. In 2014, what is the maximum contribution that a 45 year-old may make into a traditional IRA?
    a. $2,000
    b. $3,500
    c. $5,500
    d. $6,500

215. What is the maximum amount that may be contributed to a 529 plan in 2014?
   a. $2,000
   b. $5,500
   c. $6,500
   d. $14,000

216. What is the amount of the "catch-up" contribution to a traditional or Roth IRA that individuals aged 50 and over may make in 2014?
   a. $500
   b. $1,000
   c. $1,500
   d. $2,000

217. What is the maximum annual contribution amount allowed in a Coverdell Education Savings Account (CESA)?
   a. $500
   b. $2,000
   c. $5,500
   d. $14,000

218. What is the tax consequence to an individual who rolls over his 401(K) directly to a traditional IRA?
   a. The amount that is rolled over is considered income and is subject to income taxes at the individual's rate.
   b. The amount that is rolled over is considered income and is subject to income taxes at the individual's current rate. Plus, if the individual is under age 59 ½, he may be subject to a 10 percent penalty.
   c. If the individual is under age 59 ½, he must pay a 10 percent penalty. Otherwise, there are no tax consequences.
   d. None of the above. A direct rollover from a 401(K) to a traditional IRA is not a taxable event.

219. What is the tax consequence to an individual under the age of 59 ½ who withdraws a lump sum from his 401(K)?
   a. The amount withdrawn is considered income and is subject to income taxes at the individual's rate.
   b. The amount that is withdrawn is considered income and is subject to income taxes at the individual's current rate. Plus, he may be subject to a 10 percent penalty.
   c. He must pay a 10 percent penalty. Otherwise, there are no tax consequences.
   d. None of the above. A lump sum withdrawal from a 401(K) is not a taxable event.

220. What is the tax consequence to an individual over the age of 59 ½ who withdraws a lump sum from his 401(K)?
   a. The amount withdrawn is considered income and is subject to income taxes at the individual's rate.
   b. The amount that is withdrawn is considered income and is subject to income taxes at the individual's current rate. Plus, he may be subject to a 10 percent penalty.
   c. He must pay a 10 percent penalty. Otherwise, there are no tax consequences.
   d. None of the above. A lump sum withdrawal from a 401(K) is not a taxable event.

221. An individual who withdraws a lump sum from a qualified plan can avoid income taxes and penalties if the entire amount is rolled over into a traditional IRA within _____ days.
    a. 30 days
    b. 45 days
    c. 60 days
    d. 90 days

222. A transfer of assets from one IRA to another like-titled IRA is called a _____.
    a. Direct rollover
    b. Account transfer
    c. Direct transfer
    d. IRA rollover

223. Contributions made to a traditional or Roth IRA may consist of _____.
    a. Cash only
    b. Cash or securities
    c. Cash, securities, or fine arts
    d. Securities only

224. How are capital gains and losses inside an IRA reported on an individual's income taxes each year?
    a. Neither gains nor losses within an IRA reported.
    b. Gains are not reported, but losses are reported on a Form 1099B to be used as a deduction.
    c. Both gains and losses are reported on Form 1099B.
    d. Gains and losses in an IRA are both reported on Form 1099B, but they are not subject to taxation.

225. The current year's required minimum distribution (RMD) is calculated based on the value of the traditional IRA at what time?
    a. At the time of the distribution
    b. On December 31 of the prior year
    c. On December 31 of the current year
    d. On April 15 of the current year

226. By what date must an individual take his first required minimum distribution (RMD)?
    a. At any time in the year he turns 70.5
    b. By April 15 in the year following the year he turns 70.5
    c. By December 31 in the year he turns 70.5
    d. On the date that he turns 70.5

227. If a person over contributes to his Roth IRA and does not withdraw the excess amount by his tax due date, what is the excise tax imposed on the amount of the excess contribution?
    a. 4 percent
    b. 6 percent
    c. 8 percent
    d. 10 percent

228. What is the tax consequence to an individual who converts her traditional IRA into a Roth IRA?
   a. There are no tax consequences.
   b. The amount converted is subject to a flat tax of 25 percent.
   c. The amount converted is counted as income and is subject to her current tax rate.
   d. The amount converted is taxed at a flat rate of 15 percent.

229. An individual converts his $100,000 traditional IRA into a Roth IRA just before a major market decline causes the value to drop to $50,000. This investor should _____ the Roth IRA back to a traditional IRA to avoid paying taxes on the extra $50,000.
   a. De-convert
   b. Roll over
   c. Recharacterize
   d. Transfer

230. Individuals have until what date to make a prior-year contribution to their traditional or Roth IRAs?
   a. January 31
   b. April 15
   c. June 30
   d. October 15

231. What is the income limit for single individuals to contribute to a Roth IRA?
   a. $107,000
   b. $127,000
   c. $137,000
   d. $157,000

232. What is the current yield of a 5 percent bond that is priced at 80?
   a. 5.00 percent
   b. 6.25 percent
   c. 4.00 percent
   d. 8.00 percent

233. An option that is written against stock owned is a/an _____ option.
   a. Naked
   b. Covered
   c. Open
   d. Closed

234. Which of the following statements is/are true regarding the maximum profit and loss that the writer of naked option may incur?
   a. The maximum profit is the premium received.
   b. The maximum profit is limitless.
   c. The maximum loss is limitless.
   d. Both A and C

235. A stock option contract covers how many shares of the underlying stock?
    a. 50 shares
    b. 100 shares
    c. 200 shares
    d. 10 shares

236. What is the buying power in a margin account?
    a. The amount of available cash
    b. The amount of margin available to borrow
    c. The amount of available cash plus the amount able to be borrowed
    d. None of the above. Margin accounts do not have buying power.

237. How are gains and losses on options treated for tax purposes?
    a. They are treated as long-term gains or losses.
    b. They are treated as short-term gains or losses.
    c. They may be treated as either short-term or long-term gains or losses.
    d. Gains and losses on options are not taxable.

238. The price at which you can buy a security with a call is the _____.
    a. Purchase price
    b. Sale price
    c. Offering price
    d. Strike price

239. If an investor writes a covered call and wishes to close the transaction, he needs to enter which of the following trades:
    a. Sell to close
    b. Buy to close
    c. Sell to open
    d. Buy to open

240. What are option contracts that have expiration dates that extend out as far as two years called?
    a. Rights
    b. Warrants
    c. LEAPS
    d. REITS

241. Which of the following statements are true regarding real estate investment trusts (REITs)?
    a. They are professionally managed.
    b. Allows smaller investors to participate in capital appreciation and income returns of real estate without owning any property.
    c. Returns can be very volatile.
    d. All of the above.

242. What type of REIT invests in both properties and construction and mortgage loans?
    a. Equity REIT
    b. Mortgage REIT
    c. Hybrid REIT
    d. Retail REIT

243. What are the investments inside of a variable annuity called?
   a. Subaccounts
   b. Mutual funds
   c. Unit investments trusts
   d. Accumulation units

244. What is the payment structure from a variable annuity that converts benefits earned during the accumulation phase into a stream of payments for a specified period of time or over the remaining lifetime of the investor?
   a. Annuitization
   b. Income stream
   c. Retirement income
   d. Pension

245. How are investment gains in variable annuities taxed during the accumulation phase?
   a. Gains are not taxed unless a withdrawal is made.
   b. Gains are reported on Form 1099B each year, but are not taxed.
   c. Gains in variable annuities are never taxed.
   d. Variable annuities never have investment gains.

246. How is an investment gain in a variable annuity taxed when a partial withdrawal is made?
   a. Gains are treated as income to the investor and taxed at the individual's current tax rate.
   b. Gains are reported on Form 1099B each year, but are not taxed.
   c. Gains in variable annuities are never taxed or reported.
   d. Variable annuities never have investment gains.

247. Transferring assets from one variable annuity to another variable annuity is not a taxable event and is known as what?
   a. Direct transfer
   b. 1035 exchange
   c. Direct rollover
   d. Annuity conversion

248. Which of the following items may affect the performance of a variable annuity (VA)?
   a. Internal expenses of the VA
   b. Market fluctuation
   c. Political events
   d. All of the above

249. What is typically the lowest death benefit value of a variable annuity contract?
   a. The current value
   b. The initial investment
   c. The initial investment plus any subsequent investments
   d. The lowest annual contract value during the life of the contract

250. A rider available on some variable annuities that offers access to benefits before death due to a catastrophic or terminal illness is called a _____ rider.
    a. Death benefit
    b. Pre-death benefit
    c. Living benefit
    d. Medical benefit

Answers and Explanations

1. B: A person whose registration has been terminated or revoked for a period of two years or more must retake the qualifying exam.

2. C: A member may maintain a representative registration for a person who performs legal, compliance, internal audit, or back-office functions for the member as well as a person who performs administrative functions for registered personnel. A member may not maintain a representative registration for a person who is no longer functioning as a representative.

3. C: Persons who are to function as research analysts must be registered as a general securities representative and pass a qualifying examination for research analysts.

4. D: A member shall promptly report, in any event not later than 30 calendar days, after the member knows or should have known of the existence of the written complaint.

5. D: A governmental entity, an employee benefit plan that meets the requirement of Section 403(b) or Section 457 of the Internal Revenue Code and has at least 100 participants, and a qualified plan as defined in Section 3(a)(12)(C) of the Exchange Act and has at least 100 participants are all considered institutional investors.

6. D: A call is an option contract that gives the holder the right to purchase the number of shares of the underlying security. A put is an option contract that gives the holder the right to sell the number of shares of the underlying security. A covered option means that the option writer's obligation is secured by a specific deposit whereas an uncovered option means that the option writer's obligation is not secured.

7. D: A General Securities Sales Supervisor (Series 9/10), a General Securities Principal (Series 24), and an Investment Company Products / Variable Contracts Principal (Series 26) are all registered principals who may approve the purchase of a variable annuity.

8. C: Correspondence means any written communication (including electronic) that is distributed to 25 or fewer retail investors within any 30-day period.

9. D: According to FINRA Rule 2711(b)(3), "Non-research personnel may review a research report before its publication as necessary only to verify the factual accuracy of information in the research report or identify any potential conflict of interest."

10. B: The Time of Day Restriction when placing cold calls is before 8:00 a.m. and after 9:00 p.m. (local time of the called party's location).

11. D: The three General Telemarketing Requirements are the Time of Day Restriction, the Firm-Specific Do-Not-Call List and the National Do-Not-Call List.

12. C: Any gift from or to a member or person associated with a member may not exceed $100.00 per year.

13. B: A customer opening a margin account must receive the Margin Disclosure Statement prior to or at account opening.

14. C: The Margin Disclosure Statement lists the risks that are involved with a margin account – not the potential rewards. The disclosures are the following: (1) You can lose more funds than you deposit in the margin account; (2) the firm can sell your securities or other assets without contacting you; (3) you are not entitled to choose which securities or other assets in your account(s) are liquidated or sold to meet a margin call; (4) the firm can force the sale of securities or other assets in your account(s); (5) the firm can increase its "house" maintenance margin requirements at any time and is not required to provide you advance written notice; and (6) you are not entitled to an extension of time on a margin call.

15. D: The Margin Disclosure Statement must be provided to margin customers at least annually.

16. D: All of the statements are true regarding FINRA's margin maintenance requirements.

17. C: The initial purchase is subject to the Regulation T requirement of 50 percent, which equals $2,500 (500 X $10 X 50 percent) in this example.

18. A: A "Breakpoint Sale" is when an investor invests in investment company shares at a level below where the sales charge would be reduced (the breakpoint). Equities, municipal bonds, and corporate bonds are not investment company shares.

19. A: Churning is excessive trading in a customer's account for no reason other than to generate commissions.

20. D: Front running is the prohibited activity of a registered representative trading based on non-public information in his or her own account prior to trading for clients.

21. D: Churning, front running, and insider trading are all prohibited activities.

22. A: Rebalancing is not a prohibited activity, while commingling funds, guarantees against loss, and spreading market rumors are prohibited.

23. D: Member firms must disclose, in writing, to all new customers that they may obtain more information about SIPC, including the brochure, by contacting SIPC and must also provide the website address and telephone number of SIPC.

24. C: When using a hypothetical illustration to compare a variable life insurance policy to a term policy, the greatest rate of return that may be used is 12 percent.

25. A: Prospectus delivery is not a general consideration regarding communications with the public about variable life insurance and variable annuities. Product identification, liquidity, and claims about guarantees are general considerations.

26. A: The term advertisement refers to any material for use in any newspaper, magazine, or other public medium, or by radio, television, or telephone recording.

27. C: The term research report refers to printed or processed analysis covering individual companies or industries.

28. D: When making recommendations, there must be a reasonable basis, the market price at the time of the recommendation must be shown, and supporting information should be provided or offered.

29. B: Material promoting past records of research recommendations, in connection with purchases or sales, must cover at least a one-year time period.

30. B: If only a nominal sum is paid, the body copy of the material does not need to clearly state that it is a paid testimonial. If more than a nominal sum is paid, however, the fact that it is a paid testimonial must be indicated.

31. C: FINRA's Regulatory Element continuing education must be completed every three years by all registered representatives.

32. B: A U-5 must be filed when a registered individual's employment with a member firm is terminated.

33. C: The annual continuing education training provided by member firms is known as Firm Element Training.

34. B: Registered Investment Advisers are registered through the SEC.

35. A: Political contributions must be reported to the MSRB by the last day of the month following the end of each calendar quarter (January 31, April 30, July 31, and October 31).

36. C: Medical conditions do not need to be reported on a U-4. A bankruptcy, DUI, and address change must be reported promptly on the registered representative's U-4.

37. C: Advertisements of investment company products that utilize rankings must state the fact that past performance is no guarantee of future results, the name of the category (i.e., high yield), the name of the ranking entity, as well as the time period and its ending date.

38. C: New-issue municipal securities advertisements have the additional requirements of accuracy at time of sale and accuracy at time of publication. Source of data and currentness of calculation are requirements of municipal funds.

39. D: Prior to the Options Disclosure Document (ODD) being delivered, a registered representative must limit discussion to general descriptions of the options. Solicitations and trades are not allowed prior to delivery of the ODD.

40. D: FINRA's Advertising Regulation Department must approve certain options communications with the public. Options-related advertisements also must be approved in advance by a Registered Options Principal, have copies retained by the member firm, and keep records containing the name of the persons who created and approved the advertisement.

41. D: All of the statements are true with respect to options communications that include historical performance.

42. A: A municipal security advertisement that concerns the facilities, services, or skills with respect to municipal securities of such broker, dealer, or municipal securities dealer or of another broker, dealer, or municipal securities dealer is the definition of a professional advertisement.

43. B: A registered representative (RR) does not need to have a reasonable basis to believe that the customer will not need the funds invested before recommending the purchase or exchange of a deferred variable annuity. The RR must have a reasonable basis to believe that the transaction is suitable, that the customer would benefit from certain features such as tax-deferred growth, and that the customer has been informed of various features such as a surrender period and surrender charge.

44. B: CMO advertisements may not contain comparisons with any other investment vehicle, including CDs.

45. C: A member may not publish a research report regarding a subject company for which the member acted as manager or co-manager of an IPO for 40 calendar days following the date of the offering.

46. A: A member may not publish a research report regarding a subject company for which the member acted as manager or co-manager of a secondary offering for 10 calendar days following the date of the offering.

47. D: All of the statements are true. A price target in a research report must have a reasonable basis and be accompanied by a disclosure concerning the risks that may impede achievement of the price target. The valuation method used to determine the price target must also be disclosed.

48. D: A research report that contains ratings must define the
meaning of each rating; the percentage of all securities rated by the member to which the member would assign a "buy," "hold/neutral," or "sell" rating must be disclosed; and the member must disclose the percentage of subject companies within the "buy," "hold/neutral," and "sell" ratings for whom the member has provided investment banking services within the previous 12 months.

49. C: A registered principal (or supervisory analyst) must approve all third-party research reports distributed by a member. A registered principal (or supervisory analyst) does not need to approve independent third-party research reports.

50. D: Ownership and material conflicts of interest, receipt of compensation, and if the member was making a market in the subject company's securities at the time that research report was published must all be disclosed in a research report.

51. A: An email that includes an analysis of equity securities of individual companies is considered a research report. Discussions of broad-based indices, commentaries on economic, political, or market conditions, and a technical analysis concerning the demand and supply for a sector, index, or industry based on trading volume and price are specifically excluded from the definition of a research report.

52. B: A mutual fund account is covered by SIPC rather than FDIC. Bank savings, checking, and money market accounts as well as certificates of deposits are covered by FDIC.

53. A: The tentative prospectus circulated by the underwriters of a new issue of stock that is pending approval by the SEC is known as a red herring.

54. C: SIPC protects the securities and cash in a brokerage account up to $500,000 if a brokerage firm fails. The $500,000 protection includes up to $250,000 in cash in the brokerage account.

55. B: FDIC covers up to $250,000 per depositor, per insured bank, for each account ownership category.

56. D: Beginning in 2014, the basic exclusion limit on tax-free transfers during life or at death (the unification of gift and estate taxes) is $5,340,000.

57. B: If a person has made lifetime gifts totaling $2,000,000 and dies in 2014, the amount that will be paid in taxes if the total remaining estate is $10,000,000 is $2,664,000. ($5,340,000 - $2,000,000 = $3,340,000 remaining exclusion amount; $10,000,000 - $3,340,000 = $6,660,000 taxable amount; $6,660,000 x 40 percent = $2,664,000.)

58. D: In 2014, $14,000 is the maximum amount that may be gifted within one calendar year to avoid taxation.

59. A: The cost basis of securities given as a gift is the average of the high and low prices on the date of the gift.

60. C: The cost basis of securities received as an inheritance is the average of the high and the low prices on the date of death.

61. A: An initial public offering refers to when a company first sells it shares to the public.

62. B: Tombstone ads must identify the issuer's name and include the name, address, and toll-free telephone number of the person or entity from whom a prospectus may be obtained. Tombstone ads are not offers to sell and are not allowed to disclose the anticipated security rating.

63. B: The Securities Act of 1933 requires that investors receive financial and other significant information and that securities be registered, but it does not guarantee the information is accurate. The act also prohibits deceit, misrepresentation, and fraud in the sale of securities.

64. B: A municipal bond is exempt from registration under the Securities Act of 1933. Common stock, preferred stock, and corporate bonds are required to be registered.

65. B: Congress created the Securities and Exchange Commission (SEC) under the Securities Exchange Act of 1934.

66. D: The New York Stock Exchange, NASDAQ Stock Market, and Chicago Board of Options are all self-regulatory organizations (SROs).

67. C: The SEC has the power to register, regulate, and oversee brokerage firms, transfer agents, and clearing agencies as well as SROs.

68. B: The Sarbanes-Oxley Act of 2002 created the "Public Company Accounting Oversight Board."

69. C: Liabilities are not required financial information on a new account application.

70. D: Annual income, investment experience, and net worth should all be taken into consideration when determining investment suitability.

71. D: Age, time frame, and personal experience can all affect an investor's risk tolerance.

72. B: The length of time an investor plans to keep an investment is known as the time horizon.

73. B: A certificate of deposit would be the most appropriate investment for an investor with an objective of capital preservation.

74. A: A growth stock would not be considered appropriate for an investor with an objective of current income.

75. D: A zero coupon bond would not be appropriate for an investor with a capital growth objective.

76. C: Growth and Income is another name for the investment objective of "total return."

77. D: The tax advantage of owning municipal bonds is that they are not subject to federal taxes and also avoid state taxes if the municipality is in the investor's state of residence.

78. C: Investing in multiple investment vehicles within a portfolio to reduce risk or increase returns is called diversification.

79. D: An investor who invests a total of $25,000 between stocks, bonds, and mutual funds is the best example of diversification.

80. A: Speculation is the process of buying investment vehicles that have a high degree of uncertainty regarding their future value and expected earnings.

81. D: Management risk refers to the impact that bad management decisions, other internal missteps, or external situations can have on a company's performance and on the value of investments in that company.

82. B: The modern portfolio theory does not guarantee against long-term losses.

83. C: The beta of the market is 1.00.

84. A: Beta is a measure of risk.

85. C: Recommending a speculative stock to a recently retired investor who is risk averse would be considered an unsuitable recommendation.

86. A: That the investor must own the stock being sold is not a requirement for the investor to execute a short sale. The current inside bid must be higher than the previous inside bid and the seller must net all positions in the security.

87. B: Under Regulation T, the maximum amount of the total purchase price of a stock for new purchases that a firm can lend a customer is 50 percent.

88. D: Encrypted email, password-protected laptops, and printing only the last four digits of Social Security numbers on documents are all examples of information security to protect customers' personal information.

89. B: If a registered representative (RR) receives a customer complaint, the first thing he or she should do is notify the branch manager or designated compliance individual.

90. A: Firms must notify employees of their business continuity or disaster recovery plans at least annually.

91. D: A common stock would be the least suitable investment for an elderly investor who is risk averse.

92. D: A mutual fund would be the most suitable investment for a young investor who can only invest a small amount each month.

93. B: A municipal bond would be the most suitable investment for an investor in a high tax bracket who wants to avoid paying any taxes on his investments.

94. D: A retired individual with an investment objective of income would be the investor best suited to invest in U.S. Treasuries.

95. A: A corporate bond would be least suitable for a 25-year-old interested in speculative investments.

96. C: Margin in a brokerage account is borrowed money that is used to purchase securities.

97. B: Under Regulation T, the initial margin requirement is 50 percent and the maintenance margin requirement is 25 percent.

98. B: In a joint tenant with rights of survivorship (JTWROS) account, when the first person dies 100 percent of the assets remain with the surviving co-account holder.

99. C: In a community property state, when a husband and wife divorce the assets are divided so that 50 percent belong to the husband and 50 percent belong to the wife.

100. D: An UTMA account terminates when the minor reaches the age of 21.

101. B: UTMA and UGMA accounts are registered under the minor's Social Security number.

102. D: Avoiding probate, assets passing directly to the beneficiaries, and being allowed to name beneficiaries on a taxable account are all advantages of a transfer on death (TOD) account.

103. D: The authorized person(s) on an estate account is/are the personal representative(s).

104. A: A POA (power of attorney) document may be used to give a third party trading authorization on an account.

105. A: Discretionary trading authority is when a person other than the account holder may invest without consulting the account holder about the price, amount, or type of security or the timing of the trades that are placed for the account.

106. D: Duplicate mutual fund company statements are not a requirement for an employee of one broker-dealer opening an account with another broker-dealer, whereas duplicate brokerage account statements and confirms must be sent to the employee's broker-dealer upon request. Also, the employee's broker-dealer must approve of the account before it is opened.

107. C: Member firms must maintain client account statements for six years.

108. B: Member firms must maintain client account confirms for three years.

109. D: Brokerage firms use the ACAT (automated customer account transfer) system to transfer accounts electronically.

110. B: If a client wishes to donate a stock to a charity that has a brokerage account at another firm, the DTC (data transfer corporation) system is most likely used to make the transfer as it is quicker than the ACAT system.

111. D: A customer's level of education is not required as part of the requirement to know your customer (KYC).

112. D: A person who acts nervously or anxiously when answering questions about their objectives would raise a red flag when opening an account for a new client.

113. A: Multiple deposits that are immediately wired out of the account to a foreign bank would raise suspicions as a possible money laundering activity.

114. A: The USA PATRIOT Act was enacted after the attack on the World Trade Center on September 11, 2001.

115. D: All cash transactions of $10,000 or more in a single day require a currency transaction report (CTR) to be filed.

116. C: Designing a transaction to avoid triggering a reporting or recordkeeping requirement is called structuring.

117. C: Money laundering is the process that criminals use to try to hide or disguise the source of their illegal money by converting it into funds that appear legitimate.

118. D: It is illegal to tell the person involved in the transaction that a SAR has been filed. The other three statements are true. The deadline to file a SAR is 30 calendar days after becoming aware of any suspicious transaction or pattern of suspicious transactions or activities. You are protected from civil liability when you report suspicious activity. You are only required to file a SAR if you believe the activity is suspicious and involves $2,000 or more.

119. D: Officers, directors, and employees are all persons that are considered to be corporate insiders.

120. B: The Office of Foreign Assets Control (OFAC) of the U.S. Department of the Treasury administers and enforces economic and trade sanctions based on U.S. foreign policy and national security goals against targeted foreign countries and regimes.

121. D: The practice of buying and selling stocks rapidly throughout the day in the hope that the stocks will continue climbing or falling in value for the seconds to minutes that they are owned, allowing for quick profits to be made, is called day trading.

122. B: A type of mutual fund or unit investment trust (UIT) whose investment objective is to achieve approximately the same return as a specific market index, such as the S&P 500, is called an index fund.

123. A: Systematic risk, also known as market risk, affects the entire market rather than a specific security or industry.

124. C: A municipal bond is not a suitable investment in an IRA. Since the account is tax deferred, there is no advantage to owning an investment that is tax free.

125. D: Unsystematic risk is also known as diversifiable risk. It results from random events such as labor strikes or lawsuits and affects various investment vehicles differently. It is this type of risk that can be eliminated through diversification.

126. C: Tax risk is the chance that Congress will make unfavorable changes in tax laws.

127. B: Purchasing power risk is the possibility that higher prices in the future will reduce the amount of goods or services that may be bought.

128. B: The risk that a security will be redeemed prior to its maturity date is known as call risk.

129. B: A stock split is a maneuver used by a company that increases the number of shares outstanding by exchanging a specified number of new shares of stock for each outstanding share.

130. C: Standard deviation is the statistic used to measure the dispersion around an asset's average or expected return, and the most common single indicator of an asset's risk.

131. B: Treasury stock is the name for stocks that have been sold and then repurchased (and held) by the issuing firm.

132. A: Junk bonds (also called high yield bonds) are high-risk securities that have received low ratings and produce high yields.

133. D: Dollar cost averaging is the process of investing a fixed dollar amount in a security at fixed intervals.

134. B: Common stock is an equity investment representing ownership in a corporation.

135. A: Paper profit is another name for an unrealized gain. A capital gain is a realized gain.

136. C: A reverse stock split is the strategy where a company reduces the number of shares outstanding by exchanging a fractional amount of a new share for each outstanding share of stock.

137. D: An investor who currently owns 100 shares of stock will have 200 shares after the split.

138. A: If a company declares a 3:2 stock split, an investor with 200 shares will receive an additional 100 shares of stock.

139. A: If a company declares a 1:2 reverse stock split, an investor with 200 shares will own 100 shares after the split.

140. C: A wash sale is defined as selling a security to generate a loss and then immediately buying the security back. It does not qualify as a capital loss (or tax loss sale) to reduce an individual's taxes.

141. B: When interest rates increase, bond prices decrease.

142. D: Goodwill is an intangible asset that is the result of the acquisition of one company by another for a premium value.

143. B: A warrant is an option for a long period of time to buy one or more shares of common stock in a given company at a price initially above the market price.

144. A: A right is an option for a long period of time to buy one or more shares of common stock in a given company at a price initially above the market price.

145. C: Preferred stocks have a prior claim on the income and assets of the issuing firm, have fixed dividends, and are issued as an alternative to debt, but do not have an effect on EPS.

146. D: The market in which securities are traded after they have been issued is the secondary market.

147. C: Short selling does not carry low risk and an unlimited return. Short selling makes money when prices fall, carries high risk, and has a limited return. Short selling loses money when prices rise.

148. B: American depository receipts (ADRs) are dollar-denominated negotiable receipts for company stock of a foreign company held in trust in a foreign branch of a U.S. bank.

149. D: Investing internationally has all of the same risks as investing in any security, including market and event risk. It also has foreign currency risk.

150. C: A shareholder who owns 100 shares will receive $25.00 (100 x 0.25).

151. B: The opening price of ABC Corporation will be $25.09 on December 6 ($25.34 - 0.25).

152. B: The last date that ABC Corporation stock can be purchased to receive the dividend is December 5.

153. B: The Dow Jones Industrial Average (DJIA) is made up of 30 stocks.

154. C: The Dow Jones Industrial Average (DJIA) represents high-quality industrial stocks whose activities are believed to reflect overall market activity.

- 47 -

155. D: Both public utility and gold mining stocks are considered defensive stocks.

156. D: You will receive 40 shares of XYZ stock on the payment date.

157. C: The cost basis of 100 shares of stock purchased at $35/share with an $85 commission is $3,585.

158. C: The maximum taxable rate on a long-term capital gain is 20 percent provided you are in the highest tax bracket.

159. C: An investment must be held for one year and one day to be considered long term.

160. A: Assets represent the resources of a company.

161. B: Liabilities represent the debts of a company.

162. C: Equity represents the amount of stockholders' capital in a firm.

163. B: The balance sheet shows the company's assets, liabilities, and shareholders' equity.

164. A: The income statement provides a financial summary of the operating results of the company.

165. C: The cash flow statement provides a summary of the firm's cash flow and other events that caused changes in the cash position.

166. B: Municipal bonds backed by the full faith and credit, and taxing power, of the issuer are called general obligation bonds.

167. A: Revenue bonds are municipal bonds backed by the revenue-generating capacity of the issuer.

168. C: The yield curve is the graph that represents the relationship between a bond's term to maturity and its yield at a given point in time.

169. D: A normal, upward-sloping yield curve indicates that yields tend to increase with longer maturities. It also shows that the longer the time span until maturity, the greater potential for price volatility and risk for loss. It does not indicate that short-term rates are higher than long-term rates.

170. D: An inverted, or downward-sloping, yield curve indicates that short-term rates are higher than long-term rates.

171. D: An index mutual fund is the most likely to be passively managed because it seeks to mimic the performance of a specified index by holding the same stocks as the chosen index.

172. B: Duration is the measure of bond price volatility that captures both price and reinvestment risks, indicating how a bond will react to different interest rate environments.

173. B: If interest rates are expected to rise in the near future, a shorter duration would be preferred.

174. D: A wrap account is an account in which customers with large portfolios pay a brokerage firm a flat annual fee that covers the cost of a money manager's services and the cost of commissions.

175. D: The return on assets (ROA) is 5.29 percent. (18,000/340,000)

176. C: The net profit margin is 2.92 percent. (18,000/615,000)

177. B: The current ratio is 3.29 percent. (280,000/85,000)

178. B: The return on equity (ROE) is 10.59 percent. (18,000/170,000)

179. A: The P/E ratio is 10.42 percent. (49.50/4.75)

180. C: The book value per share is $44.74. (170,000/3800)

181. B: Ethics is the standard of conduct or moral judgment.

182. D: To be considered investment grade, a bond must receive a rating of at least Baa/BBB.

183. A: Calculating cost basis by selling the first shares that were bought is called FIFO (First In First Out).

184. B: Calculating cost basis by selling the most recent shares purchased is called LIFO (Last In First Out).

185. B: The NYSE, CBOE, and CBT are organized securities markets while the NASDAQ is the OTC (over-the-counter) market.

186. B: NASDAQ is the over-the-counter (OTC) market.

187. C: Chartists believe the future course of the market is revealed in chart formations. Hence, the future course of the market can be determined.

188. B: Efficient markets is the theory that the market price of securities always fully reflects available information, making it difficult, if not impossible, to consistently outperform the market by picking "undervalued" stocks

189. C: Income stocks have a long and sustained record of paying higher-than-average dividends.

190. A: Stocks that are unsurpassed in quality and have a long and stable record of earnings and dividends are called blue chips.

191. D: A cyclical stock is stock of a company whose earnings are closely linked to the general level of business activity.

192. B: Growth stocks are stocks that have experienced, and are expected to continue experiencing, consistently high rates of growth in operations and earnings.

193. C: A market order is an order to buy or sell at the best available price at the time the order is placed. A limit order is an order to buy at or below a specific price or to sell at or above a specific price. A stop is an order to buy or sell a stock when its market price reaches or drops below a specified price. A stop limit order is an order to buy or sell at a specific price or better once a given stop price has been hit.

194. A: An order to buy or sell a stock at a specific price or better is a limit order. A market order is an order to buy or sell at the best available price at the time the order is placed. A stop is an order to buy or sell a stock when its market price reaches or drops below a specified price. A stop limit order is an order to buy or sell at a specific price or better once a given stop price has been hit.

195. D: An order to sell a stock a specific price or better is a limit order. Answers A and C are examples of a market order. Answer B is an example of a stop order.

196. B: An order to sell at a specific price which is below the current market price is stop order. Answers A and C are examples of a market order. Answer D is an example of a limit order.

197. B: When the market price of ABC stock hits $35, the stop has been met and the order turns into a limit order to sell at $35 or higher. Since the market price continued to fall and stayed below $35, the limit order did not execute. In answers A, C, and D, the market price rose above the limit order price of $35. Therefore, those orders would execute.

198. A: The customer's name is not required on an order ticket. The type of order, account number, and symbol are all required items on an order ticket.

199. B: A letter of intent allows an investor to purchase shares of a mutual fund at a reduced sales charge as long as the investor purchases the total amount necessary within 13 months.

200. D: The broker-dealer is responsible for ensuring that clients receive the correct breakpoint.

201. B: Customers must receive account statements from an investment company quarterly.

202. C: Customers must receive account statements from brokerage firms monthly if there has been activity, otherwise quarterly.

203. C: A stock trade executed on Friday, January 2, will settle three business days later, which is Wednesday, January 7.

204. B: A stock trade executed on Wednesday, December 31, will settle on Tuesday, January 6, which is three business days later since January 1 is a holiday.

205. A: If an option expires without hitting its strike price, the seller keeps the premium received and the buyer loses the premium paid.

206. B: The bid is 54.64.

207. C: The ask is 54.67.

208. A: The price of the last trade was 54.65.

209. B: ABC stock does not currently pay a dividend since the yield is 0.00.

210. C: The spread (difference between the bid and the ask) is $0.03.

211. B: During the course of a trading day, when a stock's price goes up, it is known as an uptick.

212. C: Both A and B are correct. NAV is the net asset value of the mutual fund, which is the actual price, and POP is the public offering price, which is the NAV plus a sales charge.

213. D: Employees of the mutual fund company, a registered representative, and investors purchasing shares inside a wrap account may all purchase shares of a mutual fund at NAV.

214. C: In 2014, the maximum contribution that a 45-year-old may make into a traditional IRA is $5,500.

215. D: The maximum amount that may be contributed to a 529 plan in 2014 is $14,000.

216. B: In 2014, the "catch-up" contribution to a traditional or Roth IRA that individuals aged 50 and over may make is $1,000.

217. B: The maximum annual contribution amount allowed in a Coverdell Education Savings Account (CESA) is $2,000.

218. D: The tax consequence to an individual who rolls over his 401(K) directly to a traditional IRA is nothing. A direct rollover from a 401(K) to a traditional IRA is not a taxable event.

219. B: The tax consequence to an individual under the age of 59 ½ who withdraws a lump sum from his 401(K) is that the amount that is withdrawn is considered income and is subject to income taxes at the individual's current rate. Plus, he may be subject to a 10 percent penalty.

220. A: The tax consequence to an individual over the age of 59 ½ who withdraws a lump sum from his 401(K) is that the amount withdrawn is considered income and is subject to income taxes at the individual's rate.

221. C: An individual who withdraws a lump sum from a qualified plan can avoid income taxes and penalties if the entire amount is rolled over into a traditional IRA within 60 days.

222. C: A transfer of assets from one IRA to another like-titled IRA is called a direct transfer.

223. A: Contributions made to a traditional or Roth IRA may consist of cash only.

224. A: Capital gains and losses inside an IRA are not reported on an individual's income taxes each year.

225. B: The current year's required minimum distribution (RMD) is calculated based on the value of the traditional IRA on December 31 of the prior year.

226. B: An individual must take his first required minimum distribution (RMD) by April 15 in the year following the year he turns 70.5

227. B: The excise tax on an excess contribution that is not removed by the person's tax filing date is 6 percent.

228. C: The tax consequence to an individual who converts her traditional IRA into a Roth IRA is that the amount converted is counted as income and is subject to her current tax rate.

229. C: An individual converts his $100,000 traditional IRA into a Roth IRA just before a major market decline causes the value to drop to $50,000. This investor should recharacterize the Roth IRA back to a traditional IRA to avoid paying taxes on the extra $50,000.

230. B: Individuals have until April 15 to make a prior-year contribution to their traditional or Roth IRAs.

231. B: The income limit for single individuals to contribute to a Roth IRA is $127,000.

232. B: The current yield of a 5 percent bond that is priced at 80 is 6.25 percent (50/800).

233. B: An option that is written against stock owned is a covered option.

234. D: The maximum profit the writer of naked option may incur is the premium received, and the maximum loss is limitless.

235. B: A stock option contract covers 100 shares of the underlying stock.

236. C: The buying power in a margin account is the amount of available cash plus the amount able to be borrowed.

237. B: All gains and losses on options are treated as short-term gains or losses for tax purposes.

238. D: The price at which you can buy a security with a call is the strike price.

239. B: If an investor writes a covered call and wishes to close the transaction, he needs to enter a buy to close order.

240. C: Option contracts that have expiration dates that extend out as far as two years are called LEAPS.

241. D: All of the statements are true. REITS are professionally managed, allow smaller investors to participate in capital appreciation and income returns of real estate without owning any property, and returns can be very volatile.

242. C: A hybrid REIT invests in both properties and construction and mortgage loans.

243. A: The investments inside a variable annuity are called subaccounts.

244. A: Annuitization is the payment structure from a variable annuity that converts benefits earned during the accumulation phase into a stream of payments for a specified period of time or over the remaining lifetime of the investor.

245. A: Investment gains in variable annuities are not taxed unless a withdrawal is made.

246. A: When a partial withdrawal is made, an investment gain in a variable annuity is treated as income to the investor and taxed at the individual's current tax rate.

247. B: Transferring assets from one variable annuity to another variable annuity is not a taxable event and is known as a 1035 exchange.

248. D: Internal expenses of the VA, market fluctuation, and political events may all affect the performance of a variable annuity.

249. C: Typically, the lowest death benefit value of a variable annuity contract is the initial investment plus any subsequent investments.

250. C: A rider available on some variable annuities that offers access to benefits before death due to a catastrophic or terminal illness is called a living benefit rider.

Practice Test #2

Practice Questions

1. Given the following information, what is the stock price discount a rights holder would receive as a result of this rights offering?

An investor has shares for corporation XEC purchased previously at $74 per share. He or she has rights to purchase XEC shares through a rights offering at a subscription price of $82 per share, and the current market price of stock XEC is $87.
    a. $13
    b. $5
    c. $8
    d. None of the above

2. Which of the following would be found on a stock certificate?
    I.   Committee on Uniform Securities Identification Procedures (CUSIP) number
    II.   Number of owned stock shares
    III.   Owner's name
    IV.   Issuer of the shares

    a. II and III
    b. I, II, and IV
    c. II, III, and IV
    d. I, II, III, and IV

3. Corporation XEC proceeds with a 2:1 stock split. An investor currently owns 350 shares of XEC stock with a current value of $70 per share and total value of $24,500. What will this investor's position be in terms of number of shares, share price, and overall value once the stock split is finalized?
    a. 700 shares, $35 per share, $24,500 total value
    b. 175 shares, $35 per share, $6,125 total value
    c. 175 shares, $140 per share, $24,500 total value
    d. 700 shares, $140 per share, $98,000 total value

4. Corporations choose to repurchase shares previously sold to the public for which of the following reasons?
    I.   To decrease the corporation's amount of issued stock
    II.   In an effort to keep majority control over the company
    III.   To aid in funding a future merger
    IV.   To maintain the corporation's earnings per share

    a. I, II, and III
    b. III and IV
    c. III only
    d. II and III

5. Which of the following can be defined as a *security*?
    a. Fixed annuities
    b. Variable annuities
    c. Individual retirement accounts (IRAs)
    d. All of the above

6. All of the following are true of an investor's rights in a rights offering except that
    a. in the event the investor chooses to not purchase the shares offered, he or she may sell those rights to another investor.
    b. the investor chooses to purchase the shares.
    c. the investor's rights expire after 35 days due to the current market price dropping below the offering's subscription price.
    d. all of the above are true.

7. Which of the following corporate issues does an investor have the right to vote on as a common stockholder?
    a. Proposed stock splits
    b. Corporate bond issuance
    c. Election of the board of directors
    d. All of the above

8. Which of the following are true of the term *equity*?
    I.   It is interchangeable with the term *stock*.
    II.   It provides the investor with ownership stake in the issuing corporation.
    III.   The shares do not mature and are therefore perpetual.
    IV.   A corporation's goal in selling shares is to create capital.

    a. II, III, and IV
    b. II only
    c. I, II, III, and IV
    d. I and II

9. Which of the following describe characteristics of a shareholder's preemptive rights?
    a. In the event that the number of new shares proposed to be sold by the corporation causes the amount of outstanding shares to outnumber the amount of shares they are authorized to sell, the current shareholders must approve the increase to authorized shares before the sale can proceed.
    b. Current shareholders are given the first option to purchase any new shares sold by a corporation.
    c. Only after current shareholders have declined the offer to purchase shares from the corporation's new offering can the shares be offered for sale to the general investing public.
    d. All of the above are true.

10. All of the following are true of stockholder voting methods except that
   a. the statutory method involves an investor voting equal amounts of his or her votes for each of the candidates they would like to vote for.
   b. special circumstances may allow for a stockholder to vote more than one vote per share for each share he or she owns.
   c. the cumulative method involves an investor choosing to cast all of his or her votes for one candidate.
   d. there are two methods by which stockholders may cast their votes.

11. What is stock that has been authorized for sale and sold to investors (regardless of its current ownership) considered to be?
   a. Issued stock
   b. Authorized stock
   c. Treasury stock
   d. Outstanding stock

12. Regarding the results of a stock split, which of the following is true?
   a. Number of shares, stock price, and overall value of holdings changes.
   b. Number of shares changes, and stock price does not change.
   c. Number of shares changes, and value of holdings does not change.
   d. None of the above is true.

13. Corporation PPG has 22 million shares of authorized stock, has sold a total of 17 million shares, repurchased back 5 million from investors, and has 12 million shares remaining in the hands of public investors. What is corporation PPG's current amount in treasury stock?
   a. 12 million
   b. 5 million
   c. 17 million
   d. Unknown without additional information

14. Which of the following describe aspects of a rights offering?
   I.   *Cum rights* refers to the trading status of a stock after the declaration of a rights offering.
   II.   The number of rights to be issued per share will differ from offering to offering.
   III. The stock will not trade with the rights attached after the ex-date, but the value of the stock will remain the same.
   IV.   The underwriting investment bank will have the option to purchase any shares that the rights holders decline to purchase in the offering.

   a. I and IV
   b. II and IV
   c. I, II, and IV
   d. II and III

15. An investor will be casting votes in an election for board of directors under the statutory method. There are three candidates, and the investor has 1,500 votes to cast. Which of the following is an example of how this investor could cast his or her votes?
   a. 1—0 votes, 2—1,500 votes, 3—0 votes
   b. 1—0 votes, 2—1,000 votes, 3—500 votes
   c. 1—500 votes, 2—500 votes, 3—500 votes
   d. None of the above

16. Which of the following terms can be described as the day the decision is made by the corporation's board of directors to provide the common stockholders with a dividend?

    a. Declaration date
    b. Record date
    c. Ex-dividend date
    d. None of the above

17. Which of these risks are inherent to American depositary receipts (ADRs)?

    a. Risk to capital
    b. Currency risk
    c. Volatility risk
    d. All of the above

18. Which of the following describe the rights shareholders possesses?

    I.   They retain an interest in residual assets that is proportionate to their investment in the event the corporation declares bankruptcy.
    II.   They can access a corporation's financial information that would be otherwise held as confidential.
    III.   They receive a shareholder list.
    IV.   They can inspect a corporation's books and records.

    a. II, III, and IV
    b. I, III, and IV
    c. I, II, and IV
    d. III and IV

19. What is the settlement date for a trade?

    a. The date when payment is due to the broker
    b. The execution date for a trade order
    c. Five business days after trade date
    d. Three business days after trade date

20. What are some consequences of a violation of Regulation T?

    I.   On the third business day after the trade date, purchased securities will be sold by the brokerage firm for failure to pay.
    II.   The customer is fully responsible for any loss incurred due to the firm selling off securities from the unpaid order, but no other securities held in the account may be sold to cover the loss.
    III.   On the sixth business day after the trade date, purchased securities will be sold by the brokerage firm for failure to pay.
    IV.   For 90 days, the customer is required to pay up front for any purchases made.

    a. III and IV
    b. I, II, and IV
    c. II, III, and IV
    d. I and IV

21. Which of the following actions regarding stock PIX would be considered a violation for any registered representative?
    a. Rushing a customer to purchase stock PIX specifically to qualify prior to the ex-dividend date
    b. Making a customer recommendation to purchase stock PIX simply to benefit from a pending dividend payment
    c. Recommending a purchase of stock PIX to a customer by highlighting the pending dividend payment as an incentive while neglecting to educate him or her on the stock's fundamentals, appropriateness, risks, and rewards
    d. All of the above are violations.

22. What are some characteristics of preferred stock?
    a. Unless noted differently, par value for these shares is $1,000.
    b. Ownership of these shares provides a means of fixed income for an investor through dividend payments.
    c. Due to the fixed income nature of these shares, changes in interest rates have no effect on the price of these shares.
    d. Maturity dates for these shares range from 1 to 25 years.

23. The following are risks of common stock ownership except that
    a. a corporation chooses not to pay dividends.
    b. a corporation's stock price falls.
    c. in the event of a corporation's liquidation, although not last, it is still second or third in line to get paid for investments made.
    d. all of the above are risks of common stock ownership.

24. All of the following are options for an investor who possesses a warrant to purchase common stock except when
    a. the warrant will expire as long as the current stock price is above the subscription price.
    b. the investor sells the warrant to another investor.
    c. the investor exercises the warrant and uses it to purchase common stock at the warrant's subscription price.
    d. all of the above are options for an investor who owns a warrant.

25. Corporation PIX is behind on paying out a dividend on its 6 percent cumulative preferred stock. It has not paid a dividend for the past two years as well as the current year. What is the amount per share the owners of these shares should be paid to be current, and which of the following should be paid their dividend first: owners of cumulative preferred shares or common shareholders?
    a. $12 per share, cumulative preferred shareholders
    b. $18 per share, common stock shareholders
    c. $180 per share, cumulative preferred shareholders
    d. $18 per share, cumulative preferred shareholders

26. Which of the following are true of a warrant for stock PIX?
   I.   Its subscription price is set at the current market value of stock PIX at the time of the warrant's issuance.
   II.   It is a security that provides the holder the chance to purchase PIX preferred stock.
   III. As compared to a right, a warrant is more valuable due to its longer life.
   IV.   It provides the opportunity to purchase stock PIX for possibly up to ten years at the subscription price.

      a. I and III
      b. III and IV
      c. I, II, and III
      d. II, III, and IV

27. All of the following are true of the transferability of securities except that
      a. securities can be transferred between parties by physically exchanging stock certificates.
      b. a stock owner does not need the approval of the issuing organization of that stock to sell his or her shares.
      c. the secondary market is where the transferring of securities is executed.
      d. a broker dealer may assist in the transferring process of securities between two parties.

28. An investor can receive his or her cash dividend payment all of the following ways except when
      a. a corporation sends payment to the brokerage firm holding the investor's shares in a street name, and the firm applies a credit for that amount to the investor's account.
      b. a corporation sends payment to the brokerage firm holding the investor's shares in a street name, and the firm forwards a check in that amount directly to the investor.
      c. a corporation sends a check in the amount of the cash dividend directly to the investor.
      d. all of the above are appropriate ways for an investor to receive their cash dividend payment.

29. Which of the following duties does a transfer agent NOT perform?
      a. Maintains the list of stockholders
      b. Verifies owner identity in stock issuance
      c. Verifies the validity and legality of a company's debt in a bond issuance
      d. Handles new issuance of stock certificates

30. What would the calculated current yield be for an investor given the following information?
Investor buys 200 shares of stock PIX @ $45 per share.
Stock PIX is currently trading @ $52 per share.
Co. PIX pays a quarterly dividend of $1.25.
      a. 9.6 percent
      b. 2.8 percent
      c. 2.4 percent
      d. 11 percent

31. Of the different types of preferred stock, which one has the feature of enabling its owner to receive both the preferred and common dividend?
      a. Cumulative preferred
      b. Callable preferred
      c. Participating preferred
      d. Convertible preferred

32. Of the following, which describes a means for investors to obtain a warrant?
    a. Attached to a bond purchased by the investor in a bond offering for that corporation
    b. Purchased in the secondary market
    c. Issued to him or her by a corporation as associated with the investor's stock purchase during the corporation's initial public offering (IPO)
    d. All of the above

33. Which of the following economic indicators would be classified as a leading indicator?
    I.   Stock market prices
    II.   Corporate profit and loss
    III. Permits to build
    IV.   Changes in borrowing (businesses and consumers)

    a. I, II, III, and IV
    b. I only
    c. I, III, and IV
    d. I and II

34. On a corporation's balance sheet, assets minus liabilities represents which of the following?
    I.   Retained earnings
    II.   Current liabilities
    III. Corporation's net worth
    IV.   Shareholder's equity

    a. III and IV
    b. I and III
    c. I only
    d. III only

35. The Federal Reserve acts to guide and control the monetary policy of the country. Which of the following are actions it might take to do that?
    a. Alter the level of money that is circulated.
    b. Actively participate in open market transactions involving U.S. government securities.
    c. Publicly communicate its views regarding the economy.
    d. All of the above actions will work.

36. Of the following, which is the LEAST likely to be utilized by economists in analyzing the overall condition of the economy?
    a. Oil prices
    b. Supply and demand
    c. Gross domestic product (GDP)
    d. Fluctuations in the country's business cycle

37. Which measure of the money supply would include time deposits in amounts that are greater than $100,000?
    a. M1
    b. M2
    c. M3
    d. M4

38. All of the following are true of the Federal Reserve's reserve requirement except that
   a. a percentage of a member bank's depositors' assets must be placed in an account with the Federal Reserve.
   b. in an effort to stimulate the economy, the Federal Reserve may increase the reserve requirement.
   c. of the actions available to the Federal Reserve to influence monetary policy, making a change to the reserve requirement is the one least utilized by them.
   d. all of the above are true.

39. When considering a corporation's balance sheet, all of the following are categorized as *other assets* except
   a. trademarks.
   b. patents.
   c. property.
   d. goodwill.

40. Which of the following are utilized by fundamental analysts to value stocks?
   a. Company income statement
   b. Liquidity ratios
   c. Valuation ratios
   d. All of the above

41. What is the act of investors pulling their money out of lower-yielding accounts and then choosing to invest it instead in higher-yielding investments called?
   a. Disintermediation
   b. Contraction
   c. Deflation
   d. None of the above

42. A real estate investment trust (REIT) will NOT be held responsible for paying corporate taxes if
   I.   real estate is the source of 65 percent of the REIT's income.
   II.   shareholders receive at least 90 percent of the REIT's taxable income.
   III.   real estate is the source of 75 percent of the REIT's income.
   IV.   shareholders receive at least 50 percent of the REIT's taxable income.

   a. I and IV
   b. II only
   c. II and III
   d. I only

43. Which of the following is a consequence of the Federal Reserve increasing the discount rate?
   a. A slowing of the economy
   b. Demand increases
   c. Reduction in all other rates
   d. None of the above

44. The stock market will be negatively impacted by all of the following except
    a. an increase in taxation.
    b. a money supply reduction.
    c. an interest rate reduction.
    d. reduced government spending.

45. Of the following terms, which represents simply the value of a country's produced goods and services?
    a. Disintermediation
    b. Gross domestic product (GDP)
    c. Real gross domestic product (RGDP)
    d. Consumer price index (CPI)

46. Of the different types of economic indicators, which type acts to provide confirmation of the state of the economy based on indicators that occur for a period of time after a change in its direction occurs?
    a. Lagging indicators
    b. Coincident indicators
    c. Leading indicators
    d. All of the above

47. The following are M2 measures of money supply except for
    a. negotiable CDs of more than $100,000.
    b. repurchase agreements that have maturities greater than one day.
    c. money market instruments.
    d. none of these.

48. When considering the four stages of an economic business cycle, which of the following are characteristics of the expansion stage?
    I.   Decline in savings
    II.   Real estate prices on the rise
    III.   An increase in gross domestic product (GDP)
    IV.   Rise in inventories

    a. II, III, and IV
    b. III only
    c. II and III
    d. I, II, and III

49. Which of the following would be associated with the government's efforts to slow down the economy?
    I.   Reduction in taxes
    II.   Reduction spending
    III.   Increase in taxes
    IV.   Increase in spending

    a. I and II
    b. II and III
    c. III and IV
    d. I and IV

50. Which of the following are true of the Federal Open Market Committee (FOMC)?
I.   The Federal Reserve selling securities acts to eventually cause a slowing in demand.
II.   The Federal Reserve buying government securities will ultimately cause interest rates to increase.
III. It utilizes the secondary market to transact in U.S. government securities.
IV.   The Federal Reserve selling securities acts to cause a reduction in the overall money supply.

    a. II and III
    b. III and IV
    c. III only
    d. I, III, and IV

51. All of the following are true of technical analysis except that
    a. it considers a company's fundamentals.
    b. it examines past performance in trying to predict future performance.
    c. it analyzes chart patterns.
    d. all of the above are true.

52. Which of the following financial measures will provide insight into a corporation's capital structure?
    a. Acid test
    b. Working capital
    c. Quick assets
    d. Common stock ratio

53. What is the type of company whose earnings are easily affected and impacted by whatever the state of the overall economy is?
    a. Defensive
    b. Growth
    c. Cyclical
    d. None of the above

54. All of the following balance sheet transactions result in a reduction in cash except for
    a. securities issuance.
    b. paying off bond principal in cash.
    c. equipment purchased with cash.
    d. a dividend payout.

55. A corporation's balance sheet can provide the necessary information to determine all of the following except for
    a. the acid-test ratio.
    b. the common stock ratio.
    c. the dividend payout ratio.
    d. working capital.

56. Technical analysis follows chart patterns in order to predict future price performance. Which of the following are chart patterns recognized and used by these analysts?
   I.   Resistance
   II.   Cyclical trend lines
   III. Upward trend lines
   IV.   Consolidation

    a. I, II, III, and IV
    b. I, III, and IV
    c. III only
    d. I and III

57. A corporation's shareholders' equity includes which of the following?
    a. Additional paid in surplus
    b. Retained earnings
    c. Capital stock at par
    d. All of the above

58. Which of these categories of earnings listed on an income statement is the source for paying out dividends to shareholders?
    a. Earnings available to common
    b. Operating income
    c. Net income after taxes
    d. None of the above

59. Which of the following financial measures can provide a determination of a corporation's liquidity?
    a. Debt-to-equity ratio
    b. Cash assets ratio
    c. Bond ratio
    d. All of the above

60. By utilizing information from both a company's balance sheet and income statement, which of the following can be determined?
   I.   Price-earnings ratio
   II.   Debt-to-equity ratio
   III. Debt service ratio
   IV.   Earnings per share primary

    a. I, III, and IV
    b. I, II, and IV
    c. II and III
    d. I and IV

61. Which of the following is an example of a company in the defensive sector?
    a. Manufacturing
    b. Automobile
    c. Computer
    d. Pharmaceutical

62. What is a chart pattern characterized by a stock price that moves in primarily a horizontal direction due to buyers and sellers leveling out at similar pricing called?
    a. Resistance
    b. Reversal
    c. Consolidation
    d. Support

63. All of the following would be considered long-term liabilities except for
    a. notes.
    b. accounts payable owed to vendors.
    c. mortgages.
    d. bonds.

64. Which of the following would be found on an income statement?
    a. Net income after taxes
    b. Operating income
    c. Earnings available in common
    d. All of the above

65. What is the amount of a corporation's earnings that would be attributed to all of its common shareholders as dictated by each of the outstanding and individual shares called?
    a. Earnings per share fully diluted
    b. Earnings per share
    c. Earnings available to common
    d. None of the above

66. What is an order that enables the broker to have discretion regarding the timing of its execution and price called?
    a. Fill-or-kill order
    b. All-or-none order
    c. Market-on-open order
    d. Not-held order

67. All of the following are true of market orders except that
    a. they will be executed at the best possible price available.
    b. they guarantee a maximum or minimum executed price for the order.
    c. they can either be a buy or sell order.
    d. they guarantee that the order will be executed immediately upon being introduced to the market.

68. What does a buy limit order do?
    a. Allows an investor to set a maximum price he or she is willing to pay for a security
    b. Allows an investor to set a minimum price at which he or she is willing to sell a security
    c. Guarantees execution
    d. All of the above

69. An investor has sold short 275 shares of stock PPG at $26 per share. The market currently has PPG trading at $11 per share. The investor sees news of the company that may indicate a price increase over the short term. Which of the following would provide this investor with guaranteed protection against missing a purchase of PPG at a level at which he or she can still make a profit given the short position?

    a. Buy 275 PPG at $21 stop

    b. Unknown without more information

    c. Buy 275 PPG at $32 stop

    d. None of the above

70. An investor places an order to buy 250 PPG 62.15 GTC DNR. The stock closes the prior day at 63.10. Further, the stock goes ex dividend for 0.15 and accordingly will open with the market the next day at 62.95. Given these developments, which of the following depicts what the investor's buy order will be as of market opening the next day?

    a. Buy 250 PPG 62.95 GTC DNR

    b. Buy 250 PPG 62.15 GTC DNR

    c. Buy 250 PPG 62 GTC

    d. None of the above

71. A specialist can handle all of the following types of orders except for

    a. stop orders.

    b. market orders.

    c. AON orders.

    d. buy limit orders.

72. When orders have the same price, what is the order of prioritization for executing each?

    I.   Parity

    II.   Precedence

    III.   Priority

    a. I and II

    b. II, I, and III

    c. III, II, and I

    d. I, II, and III

73. Which of the following are necessary for a floor broker to cross orders, executing both a buy and sell order for the same security at the same time?

    a. The floor broker must announce the orders.

    b. The specialist for that stock must allow it.

    c. The sell order must be presented at a price that is higher than the current best bid.

    d. All of the above are necessary.

74. Under Rule 203, a broker dealer is prohibited from initiating an equity short sale for either his or her own account or a customer's unless which of the following is true?
    I.   They know the security can be borrowed.
    II.   They have already borrowed the security.
    III.   They have arranged for the loan of the security.

    a. II only
    b. II and III
    c. I, II, and III
    d. I only

75. All of the following are true of the Order Audit Trail Systems (OATS) except that
    a. daily reports are for single orders only.
    b. reports are required the same day as order receipt or, at latest, once the firm receives the pertinent information.
    c. the trail of the order is tracked from its beginning to its execution.
    d. daily reports must be submitted to the Financial Industry Regulatory Authority (FINRA).

76. Rule 80B was established to protect against the creation of a disorderly market during times of extraordinary and high volatility. If the S&P 500 falls by certain percentage amounts (within a day), all trading must stop. Which of the following is one of the percentage drops that enacts the halt in trading?
    a. 8 percent
    b. 13 percent
    c. 15 percent
    d. 18 percent

77. What is a dealer violation involving a dealer not honoring his or her published NASDAQ quote called?
    a. Backing away
    b. Pulling out
    c. Canceling
    d. Revocation

78. Of the following trades, which would reasonably justify a dealer commission above the customary 5 percent markup policy?
    a. Sell order executed by a full-service firm
    b. Buy order for low-price stock
    c. Buy order for a stock that involves higher-than-usual execution expenses
    d. All of the above

79. What does security arbitrage involve?
    a. Simultaneously buying and selling both a stock and a security that may be converted into that same underlying stock
    b. Buying shares in a company that is being taken over or acquired while shorting shares in the company about to acquire them
    c. Simultaneously buying and selling the same security in two different markets to exploit the price difference between the two
    d. None of the above

80. What trade information does the following display on the consolidated tape communicate?

PPG 43s77.77

a. 4,300 shares of PPG traded at 77.77

b. 43 shares of PPG traded at 77, immediately followed by a second trade of 10 shares of PPG traded at 77

c. 4,300 shares of PPG traded at 77.00, immediately followed by a second trade of 100 shares of PPG traded at 77

d. None of the above

81. Which of the following is true of the NASDAQ?

a. Communications between broker dealers via phone are strictly prohibited.

b. Prices are negotiated directly between broker dealers.

c. Proposed negotiation terms regarding a security are disseminated amongst all interested parties.

d. It stands for National Association of Securities Dealers Auction Quotation System.

82. Which of the following are considered to be actions falling under the role of a dealer?

I.   Charges a commission for their services

II. Participates in the trade by trading in and out of his or her own account

III. Fills the role of market maker

IV. May facilitate only the order execution for a customer

a. II only

b. I, II, and III

c. I and IV

d. II and III

83. Which of the following operates to provide quotes for those securities either not on NASDAQ or those that have been delisted from it?

a. Yellow sheets

b. Blue list

c. Pink sheets

d. None of the above

84. An investor places an order to buy 220 PPG 66 GTC. PPG declares a 3:2 stock split. Given that the order must be adjusted for the stock split, what would the investor's new order be?

a. Buy 330 PPG 44 GTC

b. Buy 146 PPG 99 GTC

c. Buy 440 PPG 33 GTC

d. None of the above

85. What does the NASDAQ opening cross do?
    I.   It is the source for what is known as NOOP, the NASDAQ official opening price.
    II.   It starts at 9:15 a.m., when trade orders are automatically executed by the NASDAQ system.
    III. It allows for order changes of only a specific type.
    IV.   It allows for order cancellations.

    a. I, III, and IV
    b. I and III
    c. II, III, and IV
    d. III and IV

86. The automated confirmation system (ACT)/trade reporting facility (TRF) handles which of the following transactions?
    a. NASDAQ convertible bonds
    b. Third-market trades
    c. Non-NASDAQ over-the-counter (OTC) securities
    d. All of the above

87. How would the consolidated tape show 4,500 shares of PPG traded at 32.77?
    a. 45s.PPG32.77
    b. 450s.PPG32.77
    c. 4,500s.PPG32.77
    d. None of the above

88. A customer places an order with a brokerage firm to sell 320 shares of PPG. The current bid quote for PPG is $5.10. Considering a customary 5 percent dealer markdown charge for execution of the order, what would be the total proceeds due to the customer upon completion of the sell order?
    a. $81.60
    b. $1,550.40
    c. $1,468.80
    d. None of the above

89. All of the following are characteristics of a stock short sale except that
    a. the position has unlimited risk.
    b. it involves, first, the sale of the stock and then, second, the purchase of the stock intended to fulfill the initial sell transaction.
    c. it is motivated by the belief that the stock will depreciate beyond its current price.
    d. all of the above are characteristics of a short sale.

90. Which of the following are true of the Super Display Book (SDBK) system?
    I.   Only a limited number of listed securities are approved for trading over the system.
    II.   It provides that an order skips the floor broker and is delivered directly to the specialist to be executed.
    III. The system automatically matches up for execution all preopening orders that can be.
    IV.   Electronic confirmation is provided if immediately executed upon receipt.

    a. I and II
    b. I, II, and III
    c. II, III, and IV
    d. IV only

91. All of the following are true regarding the listing/delisting requirements for the New York Stock Exchange (NYSE) except that
    a. the singular approval of the board of directors is needed for delisting.
    b. a minimum 400 shareholders, each of which owns at least 100 shares, is necessary for listing.
    c. notification of the 35 largest shareholders is needed for delisting.
    d. a minimum of 1.1 million publicly held shares are necessary for listing.

92. A dealer proceeds on a principal basis to fill a customer's order to buy 425 shares of PPG. Given that the dealer does not have the shares currently in his or her own inventory, he or she must buy the shares first in order to sell them to the customer. The current bid quote on the shares of PPG is $7.87, and the dealer actually purchases the shares at $8.00 per share. What is the maximum the dealer could charge this customer including a 5 percent markup for executing and filling the order?
    a. $3,512
    b. $3,238
    c. $3,570
    d. undetermined without further information

93. Which of the following securities are exempt from TRACE reporting requirements?
    I.   Municipal debt
    II. Securities & Exchange Commission (SEC)-registered corporate debt, both domestic and foreign
    III. Mortgage-backed securities
    IV. Collateralized mortgage obligations (CMOs)

    a. I and II
    b. II only
    c. I, III, and IV
    d. III and IV

94. Given the following four exchange symbols, what are the exchange names that match these symbols (in the same order)?
X, P, C, Q
    a. Pacific, Philadelphia, Cincinnati, NASDAQ
    b. Philadelphia, Pacific, Cincinnati, NASDAQ
    c. Pacific, Philadelphia, Chicago, NASDAQ
    d. Philadelphia, Pacific, Chicago, NASDAQ

95. What is the highest level of NASDAQ subscription service available only to approved market makers?
    a. NASDAQ TotalView
    b. Level II
    c. Level I
    d. Level III

96. All of the following are true of convertible bonds except that
    a. share appreciation will benefit the bondholder in capital appreciation and upon conversion of the bond to common stock.
    b. the bondholder holds a senior creditor position.
    c. they have characteristics that benefit both the issuer and the investor.
    d. they usually have a higher interest rates than nonconvertible bonds.

97. What is an investment that involves investors receiving interest and principal payments on a monthly basis as a result of individual mortgages being paid down known as?
    a. A pass-through
    b. Separate Trading of Registered Interest and Principal of Securities (STRIP)
    c. Collateralized mortgage obligation
    d. TIPS

98. If a member bank were to borrow money directly from the Federal Reserve Bank, what interest rate would be charged?
    a. Prime rate
    b. Broker call loan rate
    c. Discount rate
    d. Federal funds rate

99. Which of the following dollar amounts is represented by a Treasury bond quote of 97.08?
    a. $97.25
    b. $972.50
    c. $970.80
    d. None of the above

100. Which of the following is an example of a type of corporate money market instrument?
    a. Federal fund loans
    b. Reverse repurchase agreements
    c. Bankers' acceptances
    d. All of the above

101. Calculate the current yield on a 9.5 percent bond, having paid $1,250 for the bond.
    a. 7.6 percent
    b. 7.2 percent
    c. 8 percent
    d. None of the above

102. Which of the following is true of commercial paper?
    a. It is sold only through dealers who act as the middlemen reselling to investors.
    b. It is issued at a discount to face value.
    c. The interest rate is slightly higher than what a commercial bank would charge.
    d. Its maturities range from 1 to 150 days.

103. Which type of U.S. government security has terms ranging from 1 to 10 years, pays semiannual interest, and is obtained through a Treasury auction held every four weeks?
    a. Treasury bonds
    b. Treasury bills
    c. Treasury notes
    d. None of the above

104. Locally issued general obligation bonds are backed primarily by property taxes. A given property has a market value of $375,000 and a town assessment rate of 80 percent. What will be this property's assessed value?
    a. $75,000
    b. $375,000
    c. $260,000
    d. $300,000

105. What role(s) do corporate bondholders take?
    I.   They take on the role of partial owners of the company as a result of the investment capital they have contributed into the company.
    II.   They possess unrestricted voting rights.
    III. They have priority over preferred and common stockholders in terms of payment following a company liquidation.
    IV.   They are considered creditors of the company.

    a. II, III, and IV
    b. I and III
    c. IV only
    d. III and IV

106. A bond's yield is directly influenced by all of the following except for
    a. the type of collateral on the bond.
    b. supply and demand.
    c. the bond's term.
    d. the issuer's credit quality.

107. Which of the following bond terms represents the amount loaned by an investor to an issuer, which in most cases is $1,000?
    a. Principal amount
    b. Par value
    c. Face value
    d. All of the above

108. Which of the following types of securities are backed by the full faith and credit of the U.S. government?
    a. Federal National Mortgage Association (FNMA)
    b. Federal Farm Credit System (FFCS)
    c. Government National Mortgage Association (GNMA)
    d. Federal Home Loan Mortgage Corporation (FHLMC)

109. All of the following are categorized as secured bonds except for
    a. income bonds.
    b. mortgage bonds.
    c. equipment trust certificates.
    d. collateral trust certificates.

110. Given a bond purchased at a premium, all of the following are true except that
    a. it will demonstrate the inverse relationship between investment price and bond yield.
    b. the investment yield will be less than the bond's coupon rate.
    c. higher than par price indicates an expected higher yield than what is stated coupon rate.
    d. the purchased price is higher than par value.

111. States and municipalities may need to issue short-term notes to obtain needed financing. All of the following are examples of the types of notes they may issue except for
    a. bond and revenue anticipation notes (BRANs).
    b. bond anticipation notes (BANs).
    c. tax and revenue anticipation notes (TRANs).
    d. revenue anticipation notes (RANs).

112. Which characteristics of Treasury Separate Trading of Registered Interest and Principal of Securities (STRIPs) include?
    I.   A range in denominations of $1,000 to $100,000
    II.   A zero coupon bond
    III.   A principal portion that may be purchased by an investor to become due in full on some future date
    IV.   Selling to investors as a bundle of both principal and semiannual interest payments

    a. I, II, and IV
    b. I and III
    c. II and IV
    d. II and III

113. State-issued general obligation (GO) bonds are backed by all of the following except for
    a. income taxes.
    b. property taxes.
    c. sales taxes.
    d. none of the above.

114. What are some characteristics of Series HH bonds?
    I.   They mature in 10 years.
    II.   They pay no semiannual interest.
    III.   They come in denominations of $500 to $10,000.
    IV.   They are obtained directly from the U.S. government, purchased for cash.

    a. I and III
    b. III and IV
    c. II and III
    d. I, III, and IV

115. Which of the following is NOT required to be on an issued bond certificate?
    a. Call feature
    b. State of issuance
    c. Paying agent
    d. Dates for interest payments

116. Which type of bond issuance has no physical certificate issued to its holder, leaving the only evidence of ownership the resulting trade confirmation from the purchase transaction?
    a. Principal-only registration
    b. Fully registered
    c. Bearer bonds
    d. None of the above

117. An investor over time makes each of the following 9 percent bond purchases. Which of them represents what will be the LOWEST yield to maturity for this investor?
    a. Bond purchased at 98
    b. Bond purchased at 103
    c. Bond purchased at 100
    d. Bond purchased at 100 1/4

118. Which of the following would be the dollar price quote for a bond quoted at 93 1/2?
    a. $935.00
    b. $930.05
    c. $931.20
    d. $93,500

119. PPG corporation issues 6.5 percent bonds worth a total of $850,000. The bonds are set to come due with the entire $850,000 on August 15, 2021. Which type of bond maturity is represented with this issuance?
    a. Balloon maturity
    b. Term maturity
    c. Serial maturity
    d. None of the above

120. How are options classified?
    a. By series
    b. By type
    c. By class
    d. By all of the above

121. Which of the following contribute to the determination of a corporate bond's pricing in the secondary market?
   I.   Call features
   II.   Issuer
   III. Interest rates
   IV.   Term

   a. I, II, and IV
   b. II and III
   c. I, II, III, and IV
   d. III only

122. An investor sells short 100 shares of PTR for $42.50 per share. They also sell 1 PTR August 38 put for a $2 premium. What is this investor's total maximum gain on his or her position?
   a. $650
   b. $6.50
   c. $450
   d. None of the above

123. Which of the following are requirements for a Uniform Gift to Minors Act (UGMA) account?
   I.   A minor
   II.   Assets that are currently registered in the child's name as the nominal owner
   III. An account title stating it's a UGMA account and within which state it is located
   IV.   A custodian

   a. I and IV
   b. I, III, and IV
   c. I, II, III, and IV
   d. IV only

124. Which of the following is a type of account ownership?
   a. Partnership
   b. Trust
   c. Joint
   d. All of the above

125. Which of the following Chicago Board Option Exchange (CBOE) floor personnel are actual employees of the exchange?
   a. Option market maker
   b. Order book official
   c. Two-dollar broker
   d. Commission house broker

126. A registered representative has the authority in a discretionary account to do all of the following except to
   a. choose the type of transaction, buy or sell.
   b. choose the securities amount to buy or sell.
   c. choose to close out the account.
   d. choose the asset for the buy or sell transaction.

127. Which of the following are true of interest rate options?
    a. They can be either price-based or rate-based.
    b. They are used to profit from interest rate movements.
    c. They are used as a hedge for Treasury securities.
    d. They do all of the above.

128. What can the party responsible for the management of a fiduciary account do?
    I.   He or she may not work the account and assets in it to benefit him- or herself.
    II.   He or she acts according to the prudent man rule.
    III. He or she may have limited power of attorney to buy and sell securities and withdraw only securities, not cash.
    IV.   He or she may have full discretion, buying and selling securities from the account and withdrawing cash and securities.

    a. I, II, and IV
    b. I, II, and III
    c. I, III, and IV
    d. I and III

129. When opening an account for a customer, what information should a registered representative obtain from that customer?
    I.   Whether he or she is an employee of a bank
    II.   His or her citizenship status
    III. An estimation of his or her annual income
    IV.   A bank reference

    a. I, II, III, and IV
    b. II and III
    c. I, II, and III
    d. II, III, and IV

130. Which of the following is NOT an example of a fiduciary?
    a. Administrators
    b. Guardians
    c. Executors
    d. None of the above

131. The following are all types of trust accounts except for
    a. irrevocable.
    b. basic.
    c. complex.
    d. revocable.

132. What does LEAPs stand for?
    a. Long-Term Equitable Accumulation Securities
    b. Level Equity Asset Securities
    c. Long-Term Equity Anticipation Securities
    d. Limited Expiration Anticipation Securities

133. An investor looking to profit from movements in the values of foreign currency would buy calls or sell put options given which of the following circumstances?
    a. Indications that a country's stock market is in decline
    b. Indications that a country is headed for an economic downturn
    c. Indications that a government is experiencing increasing levels of instability
    d. None of the above

134. All of the following are true of discretionary accounts except that
    a. the registered representative on the account is solely responsible for reviewing the account on a continual basis.
    b. the discretionary authority granted to the registered representative may not be transferred to another individual.
    c. the limited power of attorney that provides discretionary authority is signed by the customer and can last for up to three years.
    d. the termination of a registered representative's employment with his or her firm also terminates the discretionary authority he or she was given over the customer's account.

135. The parents of three children (A, B, and C) would like to set up a Uniform Gift to Minors Act (UGMA) account for them. Which of the following account setups would be approved under the UGMA account requirements?
    a. The father as the sole custodian of the accounts for children A and B and the mother and father as joint custodians of an account for child C
    b. The mother and father as joint custodians for their three children under one account
    c. The father as sole custodian of individual accounts each for children A, B, and C, and the mother as sole custodian of individual accounts each for children A, B, and C
    d. The mother and father as joint custodians of individual accounts each for children A, B, and C

136. An investor purchases 1 SPX May 509 call for a $3 premium. When the option expires, the index is quoted at $522.31. First, how much will this investor's account be credited as a result of the index's current quote and the index call that was purchased? Second, what will be the net profit made from this position?
    a. $1,331, $1,631
    b. $1,331, $1031
    c. $1,031, $731
    d. None of the above

137. Registered representatives are required to regularly monitor and keep current all of the following customer information except for
    a. the customer's educational status.
    b. the customer's marital status.
    c. the customer's investment objectives, goals, and philosophy.
    d. that all of the above must be kept current.

138. What is buying and selling two options of the same class but with either different exercise prices, months, or both, at the same time called?
    a. Long straddle
    b. Short straddle
    c. Spread
    d. Combination

139. Which type of account is most often used for personal estate planning due to potential tax benefits?
    a. Joint account
    b. Joint tenants in common
    c. Individual account
    d. Family limited partnership

140. What is the premium amount on an August Treasury bond 120 call on a 5 percent Treasury being quoted at 2.09?
    a. $2,090
    b. $2,280
    c. $228,000
    d. $2,900

141. An investor with the opinion that interest rates will fall will do which of the following?
    I.   Buy price-based put options.
    II.   Buy price-based call options.
    III.   Sell price-based put options.
    IV.   Sell price-based call options.

    a. II and III
    b. II only
    c. I and IV
    d. IV only

142. What are securities that have the brokerage firm as the registered nominal owner and the customer as the beneficial owner considered?
    a. Transferred and held in safekeeping
    b. Transferred and shipped
    c. Held in street name
    d. None of the above

143. In relation to the opening of a new customer account, all of the following are true except that
    a. the principal and representative must both sign the new account card.
    b. a principal of the firm must accept and sign off on the account prior to the execution of the first trade.
    c. the customer must be sent a copy of the new account form within 30 days of the account opening.
    d. at least every 36 months, the firm must validate or update the information on the account.

144. A father is named as the fiduciary of an account for his minor child. He has traded in and out of the account with low to moderate risk securities, reinvested the account distributions in a timely manner, named the child's mother with equal discretionary authority over the account, and avoided participating in option transactions. Which of the actions named above is not approved and within the set guidelines regarding a fiduciary's duty in managing an account?
    a. Trading within the account with low to moderate risk securities
    b. Reinvesting the account distributions in a timely manner
    c. Naming the child's mother with equal discretionary authority over the account
    d. Avoiding participating in option transactions

145. What do foreign currency option rules dictate?
   a. Same side position limits are at 500,000 contracts.
   b. NASDAQ options trading is 9:00 a.m. to 4:00 p.m. EST.
   c. Option expiration is on the Saturday that follows the first Friday at 11:59 p.m. Eastern
   standard time (EST).
   d. None of the above is true.

146. An investor believes shares of PPG will rise from their current price of $65 per share. Which of
the following option contracts should he or she purchase in order to maximize their profits in stock
PPG given his or her belief in an impending price increase?
   a. 1 PPG August 72 call
   b. 1 PPG August 64 put
   c. 1 PPG August 66 call
   d. 1 PPG August 52 put

147. An investor owns 100 shares of PPG at $31.25 per share. He or she sells 1 PPG August 38 call
with a $1 premium. What would be the breakeven price and maximum total gain for this investor
on his or her position?
   a. $30.25, $7.75
   b. $30.25, $775
   c. $31.75, $675
   d. Unknown without further information

148. Mailing instruction rules as they pertain to customer accounts include which of the following?
   I.   A brokerage firm may hold a customer's account correspondence for up to 1 month if he or
         she is away and traveling domestically.
   II.   Confirmations may be sent only to the customer on the account.
   III. Account statements are sent to the address noted on the account.
   IV.   A brokerage firm may hold a customer's account correspondence for up to 2 months if he or
         she is away and traveling internationally.

   a. II and III
   b. III and IV
   c. I, II, and III
   d. III only

149. An investor would use index options for all of the following strategies except for
   a. buying calls or selling puts to hedge a short portfolio.
   b. buying puts or selling calls to hedge a long portfolio.
   c. buying puts or selling calls to hedge a short portfolio.
   d. taking advantage of market movements in terms of direction and magnitude.

150. What would be the calculated profit on the purchase of a 1 May 60 put for a $3 premium if
rates fall to 5 percent by the expiration of this option?
   a. $700
   b. $200 loss
   c. $970
   d. $70

- 79 -

151. When considering anyone but the beneficial owner of an account having the authority to enter orders for that account, which of the following accounts must get confirmation of that authority in writing?
    a. Trust account
    b. Fiduciary account
    c. Individual account
    d. Joint tenants in common (JTIC)

152. What does the Options Clearing Corporation do?
    I.   Publishes Characteristics and Risks of Standardized Options
    II.   Issues option contracts on the trade date
    III. Guarantees an option's performance
    IV.   Facilitates standardized options to settle on a trade date plus one

    a. II, III and IV
    b. II and IV
    c. I, III, and IV
    d. IV only

153. An investor initiates the following options transaction: He or she pays $2 for 1 PPG May 55 call. Translate the specific details of this options contract.
    a. Paid $200 contract premium, contract option to buy 100 shares of PPG at $55 per share, contract expiration is in May
    b. Paid $2 contract premium, contract option to buy 10 shares of PPG at $55 per share, contract expiration is in May
    c. Paid $2,000 contract premium, contract option to buy 1,000 shares of PPG at $55 per share, contract expiration is in May
    d. Paid $200 contract premium, contract option to sell 100 shares of PPG at $55 per share, contract expiration is in May

154. A custodian managing a Uniform Gift to Minors Act (UGMA) account will be bound by all of the following guidelines regarding contributions except that
    a. gifts are irrevocable.
    b. the tax-free gift limit is set at $16,000 per year.
    c. his or her authority to utilize account assets for the education of the minor is discretionary.
    d. the gift size is limitless.

155. Which of the following are true of an option seller?
    I.   Has the right to decline having the contract exercised
    II.   Enters into an option contract with the goal of having it exercised
    III. Is considered to be the writer of the contract
    IV.   Has the intent to profit as the result of premium income

    a. II, III, and IV
    b. III only
    c. III and IV
    d. I and III

156. What is a customer account that requires the account assets of a deceased party to become the property of that party's estate rather than go to the surviving party called?
  a. Joint tenants in common (JTIC)
  b. Transfer on death (TOD)
  c. Joint tenants with rights of survivorship (JTWROS)
  d. Joint

157. An investor puts together the following position:
Sells 1 PPG August 79 call for $2 premium
Sells 1 PPG August 79 put for $4 premium
Which of the following describes this position?
  a. Combination
  b. Short straddle
  c. Spread
  d. Long straddle

158. A registered representative in opening a corporate account may have to obtain which of these from the corporation?
  I.   Corporate charter
  II.   Certificate of incumbency
  III. Corporate resolution
  IV.   Corporate bylaws

  a. I, III, and IV
  b. III only
  c. I, II, III, and IV
  d. I and II

159. Which of the following is an example of a calendar spread?
  a. Sell 1 PPG May 23 put and buy 1 PPG August 23 put
  b. Buy 1 PPG May 23 put and sell 1 PPG May 21 put
  c. Sell 1 PPG May 21 put and buy 1 PPG August 23 put
  d. None of the above

160. An investor who has a long position in stock DZE would like to create a hedge of protection against downside price risk. Which of the following would provide the hedge he or she is seeking?
  I.   Long calls
  II.   Long puts
  III. Short puts
  IV.   Short calls

  a. I and III
  b. II only
  c. I only
  d. II and IV

161. An investor establishes a position involving a bear call spread:
Sell 1 DZE March 75 call for a $4 premium
Buy 1 DZE March 83 call for a $1 premium
What would be this investor's maximum total gain on this position?
    a. $3
    b. $400
    c. $500
    d. $300

162. In relation to option contracts, a bearish outlook would result in all of the following except that
    a. buyers and sellers believe that the stock price will do down.
    b. option contract buyers would pursue purchasing call contracts.
    c. option contract sellers would pursue writing call contracts.
    d. option contract buyers would pursue purchasing put contracts.

163. All of the following contribute to the determination of an option premium except for
    a. option class and series.
    b. interest rates.
    c. supply and demand.
    d. the timing of its expiration.

164. An investor purchased all of the following option contracts. Given the current pricing for each stock, which of the contracts should he or she move to exercise in order to maximize his or her investment and potential profit?
    I.   PPG August 25 call, PPG is currently trading at $24.75
    II.   HKP August 75 put, HKP is currently trading at $72.50
    III.   RPT August 81 call, RPT is currently trading at $82.75
    IV.   TJN August 63 put, TJN is currently trading at $64.25

    a. I and IV
    b. II only
    c. II and III
    d. I and III

165. An investor purchased 1 PPG August 73 call for a $5 premium. Which of the following are true regarding this investor's position?
    I.   The breakeven amount will be $78.
    II.   The breakeven amount will be $68.
    III.   The maximum loss will be the $5 premium.
    IV.   The maximum gain will be unlimited.

    a. I, III, and IV
    b. II and IV
    c. II and III
    d. I and IV

166. An investor has purchased a PPG August 33 call with a $3 premium. PPG is currently trading at $36.50 per share. Which of the following describes this investor's call position?
   a. At the money
   b. In the money
   c. Out of the money
   d. Unknown without further information

167. Given the requirements for transacting in a new margin account, what would be the required deposit for a customer purchasing 500 EXL at 2?
   a. $2,000
   b. $1,000
   c. $1,500
   d. $500

168. A representative makes two separate and unrelated statements to a prospective customer. First, in an effort to impress the customer with his distinguished educational background, he says that he graduated from a certain Ivy League institution while knowing that he really only attended that college for a couple of semesters. Second, he announces that a well-renowned biotech securities analyst is employed at his firm as of the prior day. The customer proceeds to sign on with this representative and creates an account. The next day, the representative discovers that the biotech analyst decided to leave the firm effective immediately as of early that morning. Which of these two statements would be considered a misrepresentation and grounds for discipline, given that this customer signed on with this representative based on the truth of both?
   a. The statement regarding his educational background
   b. Neither statement
   c. The statement regarding the biotech analyst
   d. Unknown without further information

169. An investor communicates to his or her representative that his or her primary investment objective is to generate income. Which of the following would be the type of investments that the representative should recommend?
   a. Annuities
   b. Government bonds
   c. Collateralized mortgage obligations (CMOs)
   d. Common stocks

170. Calculate the current yield of a mutual fund with a public offering price (POP) of $17 and an annual paid dividend of $3.
   a. 5.11 percent
   b. 17.7 percent
   c. 5.67 percent
   d. None of the above

171. Which of the following would be appropriate investment recommendation(s) for an investor seeking investments with tax benefits?

I. Direct participation programs
II. Annuities
III. Corporate bonds
IV. Municipal bonds

    a. III and IV
    b. I, II, and IV
    c. IV only
    d. I and III

172. An investor is selling 320 shares of SRN. In order to make good and complete delivery, which of the following round lot combinations would allow him or her to do that?

    a. Three certificates for 100 shares each and one certificate for 20 shares
    b. Xix certificates of 50 shares each
    c. Thirty certificates of 10 shares each and four certificates of 5 shares each
    d. All of the above round lot combinations

173. Which of the following drilling costs are 100 percent deductible for the year in which they occur?

    a. Wages
    b. Well casings
    c. Geological surveys
    d. All of the above

174. An individual is in the beginning stages of forming a limited partnership and first needs to file a certificate of limited partnership within the state he or she plans to do business. Which of the following must be included on the certificate?

I. Specifics regarding how to approve and incorporate new limited partners into the partnership
II. Educational and professional backgrounds of all partners, limited and general
III. Specifics regarding how the partnership will be dissolved, if necessary
IV. Details of the business that the partnership will engage in

    a. I, II, III, and IV
    b. IV only
    c. I, III, and IV
    d. I and IV

175. A customer would like to confirm that he or she is delivering securities according to the rules of good delivery. Which of the following is a requirement for good delivery of securities?

    a. A uniform delivery ticket must be included.
    b. Signatures of all owners must be present, and all owners must not be deceased.
    c. All attachments must be included.
    d. All of the above are requirements.

176. An investments representative has a new client that may qualify for institutional customer status. All of the following are things to be considered by this representative except that
    a. assets for an institutional customer must be at least $15 million.
    b. the client independently can determine potential investments for him- or herself.
    c. the client can make his or her own decisions based on his or her own investment evaluations.
    d. if the client meets the suitability criteria to make his or her own investment decisions, then the representative has the authority to recommend almost any investment and leave it to the client to determine whether he or she should proceed.

177. A firm representative is found to have entered a market order that was influenced by information from a report that has not been made public yet. Which prohibited practice is he or she guilty of?
    a. Front running
    b. Capping
    c. Trading ahead
    d. Painting the tape

178. The employee of a brokerage firm would like to give a gift to a colleague who is an employee of another firm. Which of the following guidelines must they abide by in doing so?
    I.   Gifts must be first given to the employers for them to then pass along to the employee.
    II.   Gifts are limited to $75 or less, per person, per year.
    III.   Gifts exchanged between the employees of member firms are always strictly prohibited.
    IV.   Gifts must be approved ahead of time by the recipient's employer.

    a. I and IV
    b. II and IV
    c. III only
    d. I, II, and IV

179. What are proxies?
    a. A type of advertising literature used to attract investors
    b. A type of absentee ballot
    c. A form of payment for securities transactions
    d. None of the above

180. What is a characteristic of limited partners?
    a. They are limited in their risk to the loss of only what they've invested.
    b. They receive compensation for any management role of the partnership they take on.
    c. They have authority to purchase property on behalf of the partnership.
    d. They are given the authority to sign off on legally binding contracts on behalf of the partnership.

181. An investor is seeking the opportunity to invest in a real estate partnership and specifically would like an investment where the overall risk is lower and where the cash flows will be more predictable and occur sooner than later. Which of the following would be a good choice for this investor?
    a. New construction partnership
    b. Government-assisted housing
    c. Historic rehabilitation
    d. Existing property partnership

182. An investor purchases a 5.5 percent corporate bond on Thursday, September 15, with a principal totaling $10,250. Given regular-way settlement, calculate the amount of accrued interest that this investor will owe.
    a. $402.46
    b. $407.14
    c. $405.56
    d. unknown without information

183. All of the following are true of the practice of churning except that
    a. a red flag for the presence of the practice of churning in an account is a high frequency of transactions.
    b. representatives churn accounts in order to produce higher commissions for themselves.
    c. regulators will analyze, along with other factors, a representative's earned commissions in order to determine whether they may be guilty of churning in a given account.
    d. regulators take into account the customer's level of profitability when deciding whether churning has taken place in an account.

184. All of the following would be considered a violation of the Financial Industry Regulatory Authority's (FINRA's) rules of fair practice except for
    a. a representative guaranteeing some profit to be made by a customer if he or she proceeds with the investment.
    b. using a pending dividend as the only reason for recommending a specific stock to a customer.
    c. the omission of an immaterial fact in relation to an investment decision by a representative to a customer.
    d. all of the above being violations of FINRA's rules of fair practice.

185. What should mutual fund sales literature do?
    a. It should utilize graphs to illustrate the fund's performance against a broad-based index.
    b. It should not contain general statements comparing the relative safety of mutual funds versus other investments.
    c. It should note the sources for any graphs.
    d. It should do all of the above.

186. All of the following are true of the Medallion Signature Guarantee Program except that
    a. it ensures that transfer agents accept securities transferred by member firms utilizing this program.
    b. it is free to members as they need only to qualify for the program.
    c. NYSE members are given the authority to substitute their signatures on securities certificates with a stamped medallion.
    d. all of the above are true of this program.

187. An investor is seeking to invest in an oil and gas partnership but would like to only consider an investment program with the lowest risk. Which of the following would provide the lowest risk to this investor?
    a. Income program
    b. Exploratory drilling program
    c. Developmental program
    d. All of the above

188. To ensure investment recommendations are suitable for each individual customer, representatives must review which of the following types of customer information?
    a. Customer's current debt load and major expenses
    b. Customer's tax bracket
    c. Customer's retirement plans and future needs
    d. All of the above

189. A registered securities representative is holding a luncheon with 25 of his biggest clients to talk about the technology sector. They are all interested in investing in the technology sector and have comparably sized accounts with similar levels of trading activity and similar risk tolerances. Would recommending specific technology stocks for purchase or sale to this group of investors be considered making blanket recommendations and accordingly be against the Financial Industry Regulatory Authority's (FINRA's) rules of fair practice?
    a. No, he is speaking specifically about technology stocks, and they are all there to hear about just that.
    b. Yes, even though they all seem to have similar profiles as investors, there may always be some way that differentiates them and thus makes the recommendation wrong for one or more of them.
    c. No, they are there specifically because of their intent to invest in technology stocks, and the representative may have specifically put this group together because of their account sizes, trading activity, and risk tolerances are almost identical.
    d. Unknown, more information is needed to determine if the representative has made a blanket statement.

190. What may a general partner in a limited partnership do?
    a. Borrow funds from the partnership
    b. Engage in activities that compete directly with the partnership
    c. Intertwine his or her own personal funds with those of the partnership
    d. Sell property on behalf of the partnership

191. An oil and gas partnership has formed, and the partners would now like to set up a sharing arrangement that would require that all of the program costs be covered by the limited partners and that, only after the limited partners have made their investment back, do the general partners start to receive payments. Which of the following sharing arrangements would provide that?
    a. Disproportionate working interest
    b. Reversionary working interest
    c. Functional allocation
    d. Overriding royalty interest

192. Which of the following departments found in a brokerage firm is responsible for determining the amounts of money owed by or due to customers as well as any dates pertinent to those amounts?
    a. Cashiering department
    b. Order room
    c. Margin department
    d. Purchase and sales department

193. Due to internal conflicts, a limited partnership is choosing to end all of its business dealings. Given a liquidation of the partnership assets, who will be first in line regarding the order of payment for those due monies?
 a. Secured lenders
 b. General partners
 c. Limited partners
 d. General creditors

194. A selling customer is rejected in the delivery of securities to the buyer of those securities. Which of the following could be reasons for that rejection?
 I.   Missing attachments
 II.   Providing no guarantee for signatures
 III. Physically damaged certificates
 IV.   Delivering securities before the official settlement date

 a. I and III
 b. I, II, and III
 c. I and II
 d. I, II, III, and IV

195. An investor is looking to participate in a real estate partnership but would like to choose a type that provides some tax benefit. Which of the following types of real estate partnerships does NOT provide tax benefits to the investor?
 a. Government-assisted housing
 b. Raw land
 c. New construction
 d. Historic rehabilitation

196. An investor seeking to invest in a limited partnership is specifically concerned with producing quick income and receiving tax benefits as a result of the partnership. Which two of the following should he or she analyze first before proceeding with the choice of partnership?
 I.   Partnership's liquidity or lack thereof
 II.   Partnership's time horizon
 III. Partnership's management, professional background, and possible track records on investments such as this
 IV.   Partnership's tax features

 a. I and II
 b. III and IV
 c. II and IV
 d. II and III

197. All of the following are true of defined benefit plans except that
 a. and employee's maximum contribution is $16,500 per year.
 b. the employer's contribution will be determined by an actuary.
 c. they can provide the employee with a retirement payment equal to a fixed percentage of his or her previous salary.
 d. they can provide the employee with a lifetime of fixed payments.

198. Which of these are characteristics of customer account statements?
   I.   They must include balances, both debit and credit.
   II.   They need only be sent semi-annually if the customer's account has gone inactive.
   III. They must be sent monthly during a year when the customer has been active in the account.
   IV.   Receipt of dividends qualifies as account activity.

   a. I, II, and III
   b. I, III, and IV
   c. I and IV
   d. I only

199. A customer receives a trade report that has erroneous information regarding the specifics of a trade execution. Which of the following would be the consequence of that occurrence?
   a. The firm is bound by the transaction as it was reported in the erroneous report due to the error being the firm's.
   b. The customer is bound by the actual execution of the trade, not the trade as erroneously reported, assuming the trade itself was executed without error.
   c. The firm is bound by whichever transaction outcome is more favorable to the customer, given that the report was due to the firm's error.
   d. None of the above is a consequence.

200. All of the following are non-allowable individual retirement account (IRA) investments except for
   a. term life insurance.
   b. real estate.
   c. limited partnerships.
   d. margin accounts.

201. For bonds that pay interest semiannually, which of the following are months when interest will be paid on the 1st or the 15th?
   a. April and October
   b. February and July
   c. March and August
   d. April and September

202. An individual is researching different educational institutions for employment while considering their ability to contribute to a tax-deferred account once employed. Which of the following is a school that would provide that opportunity?
   a. State university
   b. Public high school
   c. State college
   d. All of the above

203. An investor purchases a 6.5 percent corporate bond on Tuesday, February 15, with a principal totaling $12,500. Given regular-way settlement, calculate the amount of accrued interest that this investor will owe.
   a. $108.31
   b. $106.11
   c. $103.84
   d. Unknown without further information

204. An investor (buyer) would like to request a transaction settlement that is different from the customary T + 3, or third business day. Which of the following is NOT an option as an alternative settlement option?
    a. Buyer's option
    b. Cash
    c. Fifth business day, T + 5
    d. Next day

205. An investment professional external to a brokerage firm would like to make contact with the department within that organization that handles tender offers. Which of the following would that be?
    a. Reorganization department
    b. Cashiering department
    c. Purchase and sales department
    d. Order room

206. Internal Revenue Code 501C3 provides nonprofit status to which of the following organizations?
    I.   Trade schools
    II.   Zoos
    III.   Science foundations
    IV.   Parochial schools

    a. I and IV
    b. I, II, III, and IV
    c. IV only
    d. II and III

207. Transaction confirmations should include all of the following except for
    a. transaction settlement instructions.
    b. a statement regarding whether the firm involved was a market maker in that security.
    c. any specifics as to the type of option.
    d. if applicable, all of the above.

208. A customer has a combined margin account and would like to calculate its equity amount. Given the following information, calculate this account's equity.
Long market value (LMV): $74,000
Debit: $43,000
Short market value (SMV): $57,000
Credit: $81,000

    a. $55,000
    b. $7,000
    c. $255,000
    d. $12,000

209. Which of the following is NOT a type of defined contribution plan?
    a. Profit sharing
    b. Stock bonus plans
    c. 529
    d. 401K

210. What is one characteristic of 529 plans?
    a. They allow withdrawals to be made free of federal tax but require they always be subject to state tax.
    b. They can be utilized as a prepaid tuition plan for a specific school.
    c. They can be utilized only as a college savings plan.
    d. They require assets in the account to remain under the donor's control until the student reaches the age of 18.

211. An individual who is leaving one employer to go work for another would like to find a way to move a pension plan from the old employer to a plan at his or her new company. Which of the following are true of his or her options?
    a. If the plan is rolled over, 20 percent of the distributed amount is initially withheld.
    b. Rolling over the plan requires the employee to deposit 100 percent of the plan assets into a qualified plan within 60 calendar days.
    c. A direct transfer results in the employee not physically possessing the plan assets at any time in the process.
    d. All of the above are true.

212. An employer is concerned with adhering to the guidelines set forth by the Employee Retirement Income Security Act of 1974 (ERISA). Which of the following are decisions that would be outside of ERISA's guidelines or considered settlor functions?
    I.   Vesting issues
    II.   Eliminating plan options
    III.   Choosing plan options
    IV.   Making a change to employee-level contributions

    a. I, II, III, and IV
    b. II, III, and IV
    c. I only
    d. II and III

213. Which of the following is true of a loan consent agreement?
    a. A customer is required to sign.
    b. Securities purchased remain held in the name of the customer.
    c. Customer provides the authority to a brokerage firm to loan out securities.
    d. All of the above are true.

214. Which of the following is NOT a type of individual retirement account (IRA)?
    a. Simplified Employee Pension (SEP
    b. Margin
    c. Educational
    d. Traditional

215. Which of the following are true of a simplified employee pension individual retirement account (SEP IRA)?

I.   To qualify for an SEP IRA with an employer, an employee must be at least 18 years old and have earned at least $1,000 with that employer.
II.   The maximum that an employer can contribute to an employee's SEP is $51,000.
III. The contributions employers make into their employees' SEP IRAs are tax deductible by the employer.
IV.   In order to qualify for employer contribution into an employee's SEP, the employee must open an IRA on his or her own behalf first.

a. II and III
b. III and IV
c. I, II, and IV
d. IV only

216. Tax-sheltered annuities (TSAs) can be utilized by employees of all of the following except for
a. religious organizations.
b. nonprofit hospitals.
c. small private businesses.
d. public schools.

217. Under which of the following circumstances will a special memorandum account be created?
a. Receipt of dividends into the account
b. Long market value of the margin account increases
c. Receipt of interest into the account
d. All of the above

218. A customer is transacting in a new margin account and must follow the Regulation T rules for deposit. He or she purchases 2,000 RTN at $11. What is the long market value (LMV) of the stock for this transaction?
a. $22,000
b. $1,100
c. $11,000
d. $2,200

219. A customer with a margin account experiences a decrease in its long market value that causes the equity in his or her account to fall to 30 percent of the account's current market value. The account will be given a restricted status. What transactions can the customer still participate in given the new status of the account?
a. Sell securities and then withdraw 60 percent or less of the proceeds from that sale.
b. Purchase marginable securities by depositing at least 40 percent of their value.
c. Withdraw securities from the account only by depositing cash worth 50 percent of the value of those securities.
d. All of the above are possible for the customer to participate in.

220. An employee of an unincorporated business would like to contribute to a Keogh plan. Which of the following is a requirement for him to be eligible to do so?
   a. He or she needs to have worked for that employer at least one year.
   b. He or she needs to be at least 18 years of age.
   c. He or she needs to work at least 750 hours per year.
   d. All of the above are requirements.

221. An investor would like to have his or her individual retirement account (IRA) account moved to a new custodian. Which of the following are true considerations when deciding how to execute this change?
   a. The frequency of a direct transfer by an investor is unlimited.
   b. A rollover can be utilized only once every 12 months.
   c. A transfer is accomplished via a signature on a transfer form.
   d. All of the above are true considerations.

222. A customer sells 1,000 shares of TXS short at $11. Given a price decrease to $9 per share, which of the following illustrates the impact this decrease will have on this customer's margin account?
   I.   Short market value decreases.
   II.   Credit remains the same.
   III. Equity decreases.
   IV.   Credit increases.

   a. I and II
   b. II only
   c. I, III, and IV
   d. II and III

223. A 54-year-old individual would like to open a traditional individual retirement account (IRA). He is employed, and his spouse is not. Which of the following are true in relation to his opening this type of accounts?
   I.   He can contribute $5,500 to a separate account on behalf of his spouse.
   II.   He may be subject to both a penalty tax and income taxes on any withdrawals made before he reaches the age of 59 ½.
   III. He can contribute up to $7,500 per year in earned income to an account on his own behalf.
   IV.   He can contribute up to $6,500 in earned income to an account on his own behalf.

   a. II only
   b. II and III
   c. I, II, and IV
   d. I and III

224. A customer would like to establish a combined account with both a long and short position. Which of the following will be true of his or her margin account?
   a. He or she will need to pay the required amounts for equity minimums of the short position.
   b. He or she will need to satisfy the Regulation T requirement for both of the long and short positions.
   c. He or she must pay what is required to meet minimum equity on the long position.
   d. All of the above are true.

225. Regulation T provides the Federal Reserve Board the authority to oversee all of the following except for
    a. the amount of deposit or margin required.
    b. the frequency of credit extension to a given customer.
    c. the dates of payment for the transaction.
    d. all of the above.

226. What does Regulation S-P do?
    I.   It provides that privacy notices may be sent electronically.
    II.   It requires that a firm delivers semi-annual privacy notices to its customers.
    III. It requires that a firm delivers the first privacy notice to a customer within three days of the opening of an account.
    IV.   It provides customers with the option to opt out of having their nonpublic personal information shared with third-party companies.

    a. I and IV
    b. IV only
    c. I and II
    d. II, III, and IV

227. A customer transacting in a margin account makes the following purchase: 250 PTR at 65. What would be this customer's excess equity if the share price of PTR increases to $81?
    a. $4,000
    b. $2,000
    c. $2,100
    d. None of the above

228. A brokerage firm is seeking a bank loan and would like to commingle two separate customers' pledged securities as collateral to do so. Which of the following is true of their proposed transaction?
    I.   It requires both of the two customers' permission in writing.
    II.   SEC rule 15c2-1 regulates this transaction.
    III. It requires permission from at least one of the two customers in writing.
    IV.   The customers' securities may also be commingled with other securities owned by the firm.

    a. II and III
    b. I, II, and IV
    c. I and II
    d. III and IV

229. All of the following are true of a credit agreement except that it
    a. details an amortization schedule.
    b. describes the method for interest charges.
    c. provides the terms of customer's credit extension.
    d. specifies interest rates to be charged.

230. Which of the following are Regulation T securities are exempt?
- I. Nonconvertible corporate debt
- II. Municipal securities
- III. U.S. government securities
- IV. U.S. government agencies

   a. III and IV
   b. I and II
   c. I, II, III, and IV
   d. II, III, and IV

231. A brokerage customer would like to transfer their account from one firm to another. He or she has been notified that one of the investments within the account cannot be transferred through the Automated Client Account Transfer (ACAT) process and he or she needs to send specific instructions as to what the old firm should do with this asset. Which of the following is an option?
   a. Liquidate the asset.
   b. Physically have the asset shipped.
   c. Keep it with the old firm.
   d. All of the above are options.

232. Which of the following is a customer account document that, once signed, obligates a customer to provide as collateral for a margin loan the securities that were purchased on margin?
   a. Credit agreement
   b. Reserve requirement
   c. Hypothecation agreement
   d. Customer agreement

233. Which regulation provides the authority to the Federal Reserve Board to control customer credit in their securities purchases as extended by brokerage firms?
   a. Regulation T
   b. Regulation U
   c. Regulation G
   d. Regulation X

234. Which of the following are NOT considered to be non-marginable securities?
   a. Initial public offerings
   b. Options
   c. 45-day-old newly issued securities
   d. Non-NASDAQ over-the-counter (OTC) securities

235. Which of the following is a type of account that, for one fixed annual fee, will provide an advisory role for a customer and cover the account execution costs?
   a. Margin account
   b. Wrap account
   c. Joint account
   d. Numbered account

236. Given the requirements for transacting in a new margin account, what would be the required deposit for a customer purchasing 2,500 RZL at 22?
   a. $2,000
   b. $55,000
   c. $1,000
   d. $27,500

237. Calculate the net asset value (NAV) per share for a mutual fund with $120,000 in liabilities, $870,000 in assets, and 50,000 shares that are outstanding.
   a. $19.80
   b. $15
   c. $7.25
   d. Unknown without further information

238. The sales charge on an open-end mutual fund pays for which of the following?
   I. Commissions of representatives and their brokerage firms
   II. Printing of the fund prospectus
   III. Underwriter's commission
   IV. Mailing expenses

   a. I, II, and III
   b. III only
   c. I and III
   d. II and IV

239. An investor would like to determine the sales charge percentage on a mutual fund whose purchase price is $8 and net asset value is $7.25. What would the sales charge percentage be for this investor?
   a. 9.4 percent
   b. 9.2 percent
   c. 9.6 percent
   d. Unknown without further information

240. An individual purchased 3,500 shares in a mutual fund that had a purchase price of $23.25. Now, nine months later, upon redeeming the fund shares, the price is $25.75. What is the total capital gain on this investment?
   a. $7,875
   b. $2,250
   c. $7,500
   d. $8,750

241. An investor makes three separate purchases over six months of stock RNG, each for $250. At the times of each of the share purchases, the stock was trading at $22.73, $35.71, and $13.16, respectively. The number of shares purchased over the three transactions was 11, 7, and 19. Calculate first this investor's average cost (investment) per share and then the average purchase price per share.
   a. $41.67, $16.29
   b. $20.27, $23.87
   c. $6.76, $19.48
   d. $20.27, 25.87

- 96 -

242. Which of the following is a type of investment company as designated by the Investment Company Act of 1940?
    a. Unit investment trust
    b. Management investment company
    c. Face amount company
    d. All of the above

243. An investor is looking to invest in a mutual fund but is trying to choose the type of fund to invest in. If he or she would like to be investing only in common stock shares, have the share pricing be dictated by a formula, and be provided the opportunity to receive dividends and vote, which of the following would satisfy his stated investment needs?
    a. Closed-end mutual fund
    b. Unit investment trust
    c. Open-end mutual fund
    d. None of the above

244. The Investment Company Act of 1940 established a test in order for mutual funds to qualify as diversified. Which of the following is the series of asset allocation percents as ordered by the test?
    a. 75–5–10
    b. 65–5–20
    c. 75–10–5
    d. 70–5–10

245. An investment company is seeking to register with the Securities & Exchange Commission (SEC). Which of the following is a requirement to do that?
    a. The investment company must have a net worth of at least $150,000.
    b. The investment company must have at least 100 shareholders.
    c. The investment company must have traded at least $25 million in securities in the last year.
    d. All of the above are requirements.

246. Investment companies are prohibited from doing all of the following except for
    a. taking control of other companies.
    b. receiving broker commissions.
    c. operating with 100 shareholders or less.
    d. lending money in any capacity.

247. The board of directors of a management company is responsible for all of the following except for
    a. hiring the custodian bank.
    b. monitoring the company president and others who are responsible for daily operations.
    c. managing the portfolio of investments.
    d. deciding the type of funds the company should offer.

248. Given the following information for a securities offering, calculate the underwriting spread and the net proceeds due to the issuer.
Public offering price: $18
Underwriting fee: $1.15
Selling concession: $1.85
Management fee: $0.65
Administrative expenses: $0.35
    a. $3.65, $14.35
    b. $1.15, $16.85
    c. $4.00, $14.00
    d. $3.00, $15.00

249. Calculate the annualized premium on a municipal bond purchased in the secondary market for $1,350. The bond has five years remaining to its maturity.
    a. $10 per year
    b. $60 per year
    c. $70 per year
    d. None of the above

250. Which of the following features are common to both variable annuities and mutual funds?
    I.   Management
    II.   Taxation
    III.   Transfer agent
    IV.   Custodian bank

    a. II and III
    b. III and IV
    c. I and IV
    d. I, III, and IV

Answers and Explanations

1. B: The discount the investor would receive is the difference between the current market price of stock XEC and the subscription price offered in the rights offering.
$$\$87 - \$82 = \$5$$

2. D: Stock certificates contain a Committee on Uniform Securities Identification Procedures (CUSIP) number, the number of owned shares, the owner's name, and the issuer of the shares.

3. A: A 2:1 stock split dictates that, for every share an investor owns, they will now own two. Further, the per-share price gets split in half due to the additional shares that resulted from the split. The investor's overall position value in stock XEC, however, does not change.

4. D: Corporations choose to repurchase shares in an effort to maintain a majority interest and control in the company and to fund future mergers. They would not repurchase shares to decrease a company's issued stock in that issued stock is all stock sold to the public regardless of whether it remains outstanding or is repurchased; that is, the number cannot be decreased. Additionally, they would not repurchase shares to maintain their earnings per share due to the fact that a repurchase would reduce the amount of outstanding shares, which would consequently increase the company's earnings per share.

5. B: A security must be transferable from one individual to another and exposes the owner to risk and loss. Variable annuities are securities because they are transferable and, due to their payments being varied and unpredictable, expose the owner to some financial risk and variability in returns. Fixed annuities are not securities in that they provide for fixed payments, a guarantee on the receipt of earnings and principal, and consequently, no risk to the owner. Individual retirement accounts (IRAs) are not considered securities in that they provide for regular and predictable distributions to the owners, and thus, no risk.

6. C: Investors' rights expire only after 45 days. Additionally, investors may choose to exercise the rights to purchase additional shares or sell those rights to another investor who would like to buy those shares.

7. D: Common stockholders have the right by ownership to vote on proposed stock splits, corporate bond issuance, and the election of the corporation's board of directors.

8. C: Equity is interchangeable with the term *stock,* provides ownership for the investor, has no maturity, and is sold in order to provide capital to the issuing corporation.

9. D: A shareholder's preemptive rights provide for him or her to receive the first option to purchase shares from any new offering conducted by the corporation, provide for the shares to be offered to the public only after they've been declined by the current shareholders, and require approval from the current shareholders for any increase to the amount of the corporation's authorized shares.

10. B: Stockholders are allowed only one vote for every share owned. The statutory method provides for voting equal amounts of votes over more than one candidate, the cumulative method involves casting all votes for one candidate, and there are two methods for stockholder voting, statutory and cumulative.

11. A: Stock that is authorized for sale and sold to investors is issued stock, regardless of whether it still remains with investors or has subsequently been repurchased by the corporation. Authorized stock is the largest number of shares that can be sold by the corporation. Treasury stock is the stock that has been sold to the public and then repurchased by the corporation. Outstanding stock is stock that has been sold to investors and still remains with investors, having not been repurchased by the issuing corporation.

12. C: The results of a stock split would be a change in the number of shares (either an increase or decrease), while holding constant the value of the overall holdings. The split causes an increase or decrease in the number of outstanding shares and, accordingly, the stock's price. The value of the holdings is not affected.

13. B: Corporation PPG's current amount in treasury stock is 5 million, given that treasury stock is defined as the amount of stock once sold to the public and then repurchased by the issuing corporation. The amount of outstanding shares is 12 million, and 17 million is the total amount of issued stock.

14. A: In a rights offering, stock shares trade cum rights after the declaration of the rights offering, and the underwriting investment bank does have the option to purchase any shares not purchased by the rights holders. Further, rights are issued per share, one to one, and after the ex-date, the stock will trade without the rights attached, and accordingly, the stock's value will be reduced to account for the loss of that right.

15. C: The statutory voting method requires that the investor cast his or her votes equally amongst the candidates for which they would like to vote.

16. A: The declaration date is the date when the board of directors declares the decision to pay out a dividend to common stockholders of record. The record date is when investors must be officially recorded as stockholders on stock certificates in order to qualify for receipt of the declared dividend. The ex-dividend date is the first day that the stock trades without the declared dividend attached and, accordingly, will not be given to anyone purchasing the stock as of this date or after.

17. D: Investors of American depositary receipts (ADRs) are subject to the risk of permanent loss of their invested capital due to a company's decline having long-term effects on their ability to successfully conduct their business. Further, currency risk as a result of currency fluctuations and the volatility risk associated with stock price fluctuations are also risks inherent to ADR ownership.

18. B: Shareholders will retain proportionate interest in residual assets in the event of bankruptcy, may receive a list of shareholders, and may inspect a corporation's books and records. They do not have the right to access and review a corporation's confidential financial information.

19. D: The settlement date is three business days after trade date. The payment date is when payment is due to the broker and is also five business days after trade date. The execution date for the trade order is the trade date.

20. A: A violation of Regulation T has consequences that include the firm selling the securities from the unpaid order after the sixth business day following trade date, not the third, and for 90 days, the customer must pay up front for any purchases made through firm. The customer will be fully responsible for any loss incurred by the firm in selling off the securities from the unpaid order;

however, the firm may sell any other securities from that customer's account in order to provide financial settlement for the loss.

21. D: A registered representative would be committing a violation by rushing a customer to make a purchase solely to meet the ex-dividend date, recommending a purchase simply to benefit from a pending dividend, or promoting a stock by highlighting the benefit of the pending dividend while neglecting to educate him or her as to the fundamentals or appropriateness this stock may have as an investment.

22. B: Ownership in preferred stock provides a fixed income to the investor through dividend payments. The par value of shares is generally $100, not $1,000. Due to the fixed income nature of these shares, they are more sensitive to changes in interest rates, demonstrating an inverse relationship between rates and pricing. These shares have no maturity date and are therefore considered perpetual.

23. C: In the event of a corporation's liquidation, common stockholders are paid last, not second or third, in the line of other creditors and investors. Other risks include no payout of stock dividend and the fall of the stock price.

24. A: The warrant will expire when the current stock price is below the subscription price of the warrant. The investor may also sell the warrant to another investor or exercise the warrant in order to purchase common stock at the subscription price.

25. D:

$$3 \times \$6 = \$18 \text{ per share}$$

Cumulative preferred shareholders always have priority over common stock shareholders in terms of dividend payment. They must receive both the missed dividend amounts as well as the current year's before PIX can pay any dividend to its common shareholders.

26. B: A warrant for stock PIX would be more valuable than a right due to its longer life and would provide the opportunity to purchase stock PIX for possibly up to 10 years at the subscription price. Its subscription price, however, is set above the current market value of stock PIX at the time of the warrant's issuance, and further, the warrant provides the holder the chance to purchase PIX common stock, not preferred.

27. A: Securities are transferable only after the owner either endorses the stock certificates or signs a power of substitution into the new owner's name. Owners may sell shares without the approval of the requisite issuing organization, securities transfers are executed in the secondary market, and broker dealers assist in the securities transferring process.

28. B: In the event a corporation pays a cash dividend to investors, an investor may receive that payment as a credit to his or her brokerage account as applied by the brokerage firm or as a check for that amount sent directly to him or her from the corporation paying the dividend. A brokerage firm holding the shares in a street name would not send the investor a check in that amount directly.

29. C: A transfer agent does not verify company debt; this is the role of the registrar. A transfer agent does maintain the list of stockholders, verifies the correct issuance of shares, and handles the new issuance of stock certificates.

30. A:

$$\text{current yield} = \frac{\text{annual income}}{\text{current market price}}$$

$$\text{current yield} = \frac{(1.25 \times 4)}{52} = 0.096 = 9.6\%$$

31. C: Participating preferred stock ownership provides the investor the right to receive both the preferred and common dividend when paid. Cumulative preferred shares not only allow the owner payment of the preferred dividend but also provide protection against missed dividend payments by requiring back payment of those dividends. Callable shares afford the corporation the right to call in those shares, often at a premium price. Convertible shares allow for the option to exchange preferred shares for common shares at a conversion price.

32. D: An investor may obtain a warrant as attached to a bond purchased in a bond offering, purchased in the secondary market, or issued to him or her due to participation in a corporation's initial public offering (IPO).

33. C: Stock market prices, permits for building, and changes in business and consumer borrowing are all considered to be leading economic indicators in that they each act as signals of an impending change to the economy and, accordingly, can be observed prior to the actual change. Corporate profits and losses are considered to be lagging economic indicators in that these types of effects are more observable after the change in the economy has already occurred.

34. A: On a corporation's balance sheet, assets minus liabilities represents both the corporation's net worth and its shareholders' equity. A corporation's retained earnings are the balance of net income beyond what may be paid out as dividends. Current liabilities are the financial obligations of the corporation that come due within the next 12 months.

35. D: The Federal Reserve may alter the level of money in circulation, actively transact in U.S. government securities in the open market, and publicly share its views on the economy and the direction it sees it taking.

36. A: In analyzing the overall condition of a country's economy, an economist would be least likely to utilize oil prices, and MORE likely to look to charts and models regarding supply and demand, the country's gross domestic product (GDP), and fluctuations in its business cycle.

37. C: The measure of money supply that includes time deposits greater than $100,000 is M3. It also includes all the measures in M1 and M2.

38. B: The Federal Reserve, in attempting to stimulate the economy, would reduce the reserve requirement, not increase it. Reducing it would allow for an increase in banks' abilities to lend, a reduction in interest rates, increase in demand, and ultimately, the economy being stimulated. The reserve requirement involves a percentage of a member bank's depositors' assets to be placed in an account with the Federal Reserve. Further, altering the reserve requirement is the least utilized action to influence monetary policy that the Federal Reserve has at its disposal.

39. C: Property, when categorized on a corporation's balance sheet, is considered a fixed asset. Other assets can include a corporation's trademarks, patents, and goodwill.

40. D: Fundamental analysts will refer to company income statements, liquidity ratios, and valuation ratios in trying to determine a stock's value.

41. A: Disintermediation involves investors moving their money from low-yielding accounts to higher-yielding ones. A contraction occurs when gross domestic product (GDP) and the stock market fall, while unemployment rises. Deflation is an economic condition that results from a decrease in demand for goods and services and consequently involves a decrease in prices for those same goods and services.

42. C: A real estate investment trust (REIT) will NOT be held responsible for paying corporate taxes if their shareholders receive at least 90 percent of the REIT's taxable income, and real estate is the source of 75 percent of the REIT's income.

43. A: If the Federal Reserve were to increase the discount rate, all other rates would go up, demand would decrease, and ultimately, the economy would be slowed.

44. C: Falling interest rates will have a positive effect on stock market performance. An increase in taxes, or a reduction in the money supply or government spending, will negatively impact the stock market.

45. B: The value of a country's produced goods and services is its gross domestic product (GDP). Disintermediation involves investors moving their money from low-yielding investments to higher-yielding ones. The real GDP is a deflation- and inflation-adjusted version of the value of a country's produced goods and services. The consumer price index (CPI) is a tool utilized to measure the rise and fall of overall prices in the country by monitoring the price changes of a specific group of goods and services chosen for their high degree of use in individual lives.

46. A: Lagging indicators take effect after the new direction of economy takes effect, take hold for a period of time, and provide confirmation about that change. Coincident indicators are an immediate result of even slight changes in the economy. Leading indicators occur prior to the economic change and can be looked to in order to analyze the future state of the economy.

47. B: Repurchase agreements with maturities of greater than one day would be categorized as M3, not M2. Negotiable CDs of more than $100,000 and money market instruments are both considered M2 money supply measures.

48. C: With regards to the stages of an economic business cycle, the expansion stage would be characterized by a rise in real estate prices and an increase in gross domestic product (GDP). A decline in the amount and rate of savings and a rise in inventories would be characteristics of the contraction stage.

49. B: The government, in moving to slow down the economy, would reduce spending and increase taxes so as to reduce overall demand for goods and services and decrease the level of money that consumers have access to.

50. D: The Federal Open Market Committee (FOMC) does utilize the secondary market to transact in U.S. government securities. Further, the Federal Reserve selling securities acts to both reduce the overall money supply and slow demand. However, the Federal Reserve buying government

securities will ultimately cause interest rates to decrease due to the resulting increase in the money available to lend.

51. A: Technical analysis does not consider a company's fundamentals in its attempt to predict price performance. Instead, a technical analyst will examine chart patterns of past price performance in order to predict the direction and magnitude of future price performance.

52. D: The results of a common stock ratio calculation will provide insight into a corporation's capital structure. An acid test, working capital, or quick assets calculation will help in determining a corporation's liquidity position.

53. C: A cyclical company is sensitive to the current state of the overall economy and reflects whatever that may be during periods of both high and low performance. A company in a defensive industry is the least sensitive to the state of the overall economy. A company in a growth industry will see faster growth than whatever the current state of the overall economy is.

54. A: A securities issuance would result in an increase in a corporation's cash by the amount gained in the offering, net other costs. Paying off bond principles in cash, buying equipment with cash, and a dividend payout would all result in a reduction in a corporation's cash position.

55. C: A corporation's dividend payout ratio can be determined using both the balance sheet and the income statement. Using only the balance sheet, one could calculate an acid-test ratio, a common stock ratio, and the corporation's working capital amount.

56. B: Chart patterns recognized and utilized by technical analysts in charting price performance are resistance, upward trend lines, and consolidation.

57. D: Shareholders' equity is made up of additional paid in surplus, retained earnings, and capital stock at par.

58. C: The earnings category on the income statement that provides the source for paying out dividends to shareholders is net income after taxes.

59. B: The cash assets ratio will provide a corporation's liquidity position. The debt-to-equity ratio and bond ratio will both provide insight into a corporation's capital structure.

60. A: Utilizing information from a company's balance sheet and income statement, the price-earnings ratio, debt service ratio, and earnings per share primary can be calculated. The debt-to-equity ratio can be calculated using only information from the balance sheet.

61. D: A pharmaceutical company would be categorized as defensive, providing products that are needed and will be purchased by individuals regardless of the state of the economy. Manufacturing and automobile companies would be cyclical, and a computer company would be growth.

62. C: A primarily horizontal chart pattern with buyers and sellers establishing pricing at similar levels is called consolidation. A resistance pattern is established after price appreciation occurs, causing ample sellers and supply, which then prevent further price increases. A reversal pattern occurs when the price of a stock has a drastic change in direction and activity. A support pattern is established as a result of price depreciation bringing additional interest, buyers, and demand, which then prevent further price decreases.

63. B: Accounts payable that are owed to a corporation's vendors are considered to be current liabilities, not long-term liabilities. They must be paid within 12 months. Notes, mortgages, and bonds are all long-term liabilities and are due to be paid by the corporation after 12 months.

64. D: The income statement would list a corporation's net income after taxes, operating income, and earnings available in common.

65. B: Earnings per share are the amount of a corporation's earnings owed to its common shareholders as divided by each of the outstanding common shares. Earnings per share fully diluted are a corporation's earnings attributed to each individual share after the conversion of any convertible securities. Earnings available in common are the amount of earnings available to common shareholders after taxes and the payout of any preferred dividend.

66. D: A not-held order gives discretion to the broker as to timing and price for the order's execution. A fill-or-kill order must be executed immediately upon receipt, or it must be cancelled. An all-or-none order indicates that the investor would like all of the securities bought or sold in the transaction or none at all. A market-on-open order indicates the investor's wish to have it executed right at the opening of the market or as close to it as possible.

67. B: Market orders do NOT guarantee a maximum or minimum executed price and in fact do not guarantee any specific price at all. Market orders can either be for a buy or sell order and are guaranteed to be filled immediately upon being introduced to the market and at the best possible price available.

68. A: A buy limit order allows protection to an investor by providing the chance to set a maximum price they are willing to pay for a security. A sell limit order allows an investor to set a minimum price at which he or she is willing to sell a security. A buy limit order provides price protection to the investor in that it guarantees he or she will not pay over a certain price for that security, but accordingly, it will NOT guarantee execution of that order in the event that the price level of that security does not reach the investor's desired price or below.

69. A: A buy 275 PPG at $21 stop order will allow this investor to pay no more than $21 per share in filling the short position, which has a sell price of $26 per share. A profit will still be made. Conversely, a buy 275 PPG at $32 stop order will enable their order to go as high as $32 a share before being executed, thus potentially eliminating a profit being made by this investor on the short position.

70. B: The investor's order will be to buy 250 PPG 62.15 GTC DNR. The buy order remains exactly the same due to the investor stipulating the order to be do not reduce (DNR), and accordingly, the order will not be reduced to reflect the distribution of dividends.

71. B: A specialist cannot accept market orders in that the nature of those types of orders dictates that they be executed as soon as they are presented to the market, and accordingly, there would be at that point no order to leave with the specialist.

72. C: When orders come in at the same price, they are filled based on priority (first in, first executed), precedence (the larger of the orders is executed first), and parity (if all orders are the same, outstanding orders and shares are divided and shared).

73. D: In order for a floor broker to execute cross orders for the same stock at the same time, the specialist for that stock first must allow it, the floor broker must announce the orders, and the sell order must be presented at a price higher than the current best bid on that stock.

74. C: Under Rule 203, a broker dealer cannot initiate an equity short sale transaction unless he or she has already borrowed the security, he or she has arranged to borrow the security, or he or she reasonably believes he or she can borrow the security.

75. A: Daily Order Audit Trail Systems (OATS) reports are for both single and multiple orders. OATS track the trail of a trade from its beginning to end, daily OATS reports must be submitted to the Financial Industry Regulatory Authority (FINRA), and reports are required the same day as receipt of the order or as soon as the firm receives the necessary information.

76. B: Rule 80B goes into effect following the S&P 500 dropping by 7, 13, or 20 percent within a day of trading.

77. A: Once quotes are published over the NASDAQ workstation, they must be honored. They are considered to be firm quotes, and a dealer refusing to honor his or her firm quotes is committing a violation known as backing away.

78. D: In justifying a dealer's higher-than-customary 5 percent commission, he or she would point to transactions that involve stocks due to the higher risk versus bonds and those trades that involve higher-than-usual execution expenses. Further, the dealer, being a full-service firm, may also be justification for the higher commission charge.

79. A: Security arbitrage involves the simultaneous purchase and sale of both a stock and a security that may be converted into that same underlying stock. Buying shares in a company that is being taken over or acquired, while shorting shares in the company about to acquire them, is risk arbitrage. Simultaneously buying and selling the same security in two different markets in order to exploit the price difference between the two is market arbitrage.

80. C: The trade communicated by the display of *PPG 43s77.77* would be 4,300 shares of PPG traded at 77, immediately followed by a second trade of 100 shares of PPG traded at 77.

81. B: The NASDAQ is a negotiated market where security prices are negotiated directly between broker dealers. Communications between the dealers may be via phone, and any negotiated terms regarding a given security are kept between the two negotiating parties only. Last, NASDAQ stands for National Association of Securities Dealers Automated Quotation System.

82. D: Actions falling under the role of a dealer include participating in trades by trading in and out of his or her own account, such as using securities in the account to fill a buy order or buying securities for the account to fill a customer's sell order. Further, making a market in a security is also an action performed by a dealer. Conversely, a broker simply facilitates order execution for a customer, while not participating in the transaction, and charges a commission for their services.

83. C: The pink sheets is an electronic marketplace that acts to provide quotes for securities that are either not listed on NASDAQ or those that have been delisted from it. Yellow sheets is a publication generated daily that provides corporate bond quotes. The blue list is a publication generated daily that provides offerings involving municipal bonds.

84. A: Once adjusted for the 3:2 stock split, the investor's new order would be buying 330 PPG 44 GTC.

85. B: The NASDAQ opening cross is the source for the NASDAQ official opening price (NOOP) and allows only order changes that are more aggressive in type, such as increasing the size of the order. It begins at 9:28 a.m., not 9:15 a.m., and does NOT allow for order cancellations of any kind.

86. D: The automated confirmation system (ACT)/trade reporting facility (TRF) provides reporting for trades and includes NASDAQ convertible bonds, third-market trades, and non-NASDAQ over-the-counter (OTC) securities.

87. A: The consolidated tape would display the trade as 45s.PPG32.77.

88. B:
$$1.00 - 0.95 = 0.05 = 5\%$$

$$5.10 \times 0.95 = \$4.845 \text{ proceeds per share sold}$$

$$4.845 \times 320 = \$1,550.40 \text{ total proceeds after execution of the sell order}$$

89. D: A short sale transaction involves first the sale of a stock and, second, a buy transaction intended to fulfill the initial sell transaction. The motivating belief in initiating this position is that the stock price will depreciate, offering the short seller the opportunity to purchase the stock at a lower price than sold in the short sale. The risk in this position is unlimited in that the price of the stock has the unlimited potential to rise beyond the sale price received.

90. C: The Super Display Book (SDBK) system provides for an order to skip past the floor broker and be delivered directly to the specialist for execution, automatically matches up all preopening orders to be executed that can be, and provides for an electronic confirmation if executed immediately upon receipt. All listed securities may be traded over the system.

91. A: In order for a stock to be delisted from the New York Stock Exchange (NYSE), the approval of both the company's board of directors and the board's audit committee are necessary. Additionally, delisting requires notification of the company's 35 largest shareholders. Listing requires a minimum of 400 shareholders each owning at least 100 shares and a minimum of 1.1 million publicly held shares.

92. C:
$$1.00 + 0.05 = 1.05 = 105\%$$

$$8.00 \times 1.05 = \$8.40 \text{ cost per share}$$

$$8.4 \times 425 = \$3,570 \text{ total cost charged to customer}$$

When a dealer fills an order on a principal basis, it is considered a riskless principal transaction. He or she does not own the shares in inventory and therefore must go out and buy them only then to turn around and sell them in order to fill the customer's buy order. Given that, the 5 percent markup charged to the customer for this order will be based on the dealer's actual cost per share, not the current market bid price per share.

93. C: The Trade Reporting and Compliance Engine (TRACE) system reports the transactions of fixed-income securities that are eligible for reporting. Securities that are exempt include municipal debt, mortgage-backed securities, and collateralized mortgage obligations (CMOs). Securities & Exchange Commission (SEC)-registered corporate debt transactions, domestic and foreign, must be reported through the TRACE system.

94. B: The exchange names that match X, P, C, and Q are Philadelphia, Pacific, Cincinnati, and NASDAQ.

95. D: The highest level of service for a NASDAQ subscription is level III. NASDAQ TotalView is a quotation service covering all securities traded over NASDAQ. Level II is provided to order-entry firms and enables them to view the quotes associated with all market makers and allows for order execution. Level I offers the lowest level of service and provides quotes for registered representatives.

96. D: Convertible bonds usually pay a lower interest rate versus nonconvertible bonds due to the convertible feature of the bond. The lower rate of interest benefits the corporate issuer of the bond in reducing the interest expense he or she pays over the life of the bond. Share appreciation could result in capital appreciation in the bond price for the bondholder and further appreciation upon conversion of the bond to common stock. Finally, the bondholder holds a senior position as a creditor of the corporation.

97. A: Pass-throughs provide investors with interest and principal payment income relative to their initial investments in pools of mortgages. The payments flow through to them on a monthly basis as the individual mortgages in the pools are paid down. A Separate Trading of Registered Interest and Principal of Securities (STRIP) is an investment that provides the opportunity to purchase separately either the principal or interest payment cash flow stream of a Treasury security. Collateralized mortgage obligations (CMOs) are similar to pass-throughs except that they are separated into different maturity schedules, or tranches, each being paid in full one at a time. Treasury inflation protected securities (TIPS) are securities whose interest payments and principal amounts are influenced by the level and movement of inflation.

98. C: A member bank borrowing money directly from the Federal Reserve Bank would be charged the discount rate on the borrowed funds. The prime rate is the rate banks charge their corporate customers with the best credit. The broker call loan rate is the rate that broker dealers are charged by banks to finance margin purchases made by their customers. The federal funds rate is charged by member banks to each other for overnight loans.

99. B: Treasury bonds are quoted as a percentage of par and, accordingly, in terms of 32nds of 1 percent. Here, 97.08 translates to 97 8/32 percent.

$$97.08 = 97 \ 8/32 \ \% = 97.25\%$$

$$0.9725 \times \$1,000 = \$972.50$$

100. D: All of the above are types of corporate money market instruments. Federal fund loans are made between banks, short term in length, and for $1 million or more. Reverse repurchase agreements involve an institutional investor selling securities to a dealer with the intention of repurchasing them back at a later date. Bankers' acceptances are like postdated checks, to provide payment to whomever brings them to the issuing bank for processing on the stated due dates.

101. A:

$$\text{current yield} = \frac{\text{bond's annual income}}{\text{current market price}}$$

$$\text{annual income} = \text{coupon rate} \times \text{par value of the bond}$$

$$9.5\% = 0.095$$

$$\text{annual income} = 0.095 \times \$1{,}000 = \$95$$

$$\text{current yield} = \frac{\$95}{\$1{,}250} = 0.076 = 7.6\%$$

102. B: Commercial paper is issued at a discount to face value. It is issued in two ways, direct paper and dealer paper. In the former, the sale is made without the use of a dealer, and in the latter, the paper is sold to dealers who then resell it to investors. The interest rate for commercial paper is actually lower than what a commercial bank would charge, and the maturities range from 1 to 270 days.

103. C: Treasury notes have terms ranging from 1 to 10 years, pay semiannual interest, and are obtained through a Treasury auction held every four weeks. Treasury bonds have maturities ranging from 10 to 30 years. Treasury bills have maturities ranging from 4 to 52 weeks, do not pay semiannual interest, and are obtained through a weekly Treasury auction.

104. D: In the determination of property value in relation to assessments and general obligation bonds, a property's value will not be its market value, but instead, its assessed value will be determined using the local assessment rate.

$$80\% = 0.80$$

$$\$375{,}000 \times 0.80 = \$300{,}000$$

105. D: Corporate bondholders are considered to be creditors of the company, not owners. They only possess voting rights in the event the company fails in its ability to deliver timely interest and principal payments to them and take priority over preferred and common stockholders when owed funds that result from a company liquidation.

106. B: A bond's yield is not directly influenced or determined by the concept of supply and demand. It is influenced by the type of collateral on the bond, the bond's term, and the issuer's credit quality.

107. D: The amount loaned to an issuer by an investor, which in most cases is $1,000, can be described as the principal amount, par value, or face value of the bond.

108. C: Government National Mortgage Association (GNMA) securities are backed by the full faith and credit of the U.S. government. Federal National Mortgage Association (FNMA) is a public for-profit corporation in the business of purchasing mortgages and then bundling them to create mortgage-backed securities. Federal Farm Credit System (FFCS) is made up of privately owned

lenders who sell securities that are backed by their own obligations. Federal Home Loan Mortgage Corporation (FHLMC) is a publicly traded company that purchases residential mortgages and bundles them into pools in order to then sell off interest in them to investors.

109. A: Income bonds are considered to be unsecured bonds in that interest will only be paid to the investor if the corporate issuer has the income to do it. Mortgage bonds, equipment trust certificates, and collateral trust certificates are considered to be secured bonds in that they are all backed by a specific type of asset as collateral.

110. C: The investment purchase price of bonds and their yields demonstrate an inverse relationship in that, as prices rise, yields fall. Therefore, a higher than par price will not indicate an expected higher yield than what is the stated coupon rate. A bond purchased at a premium indicates a purchase price paid that is above par and, consequently, an expected investment yield that will be less than the bond's coupon rate.

111. A: The types of short-term notes that a municipality or state may issue include bond anticipation notes (BANs), tax and revenue anticipation notes (TRANs), and revenue anticipation notes (RANs).

112. D: Treasury Separate Trading of Registered Interest and Principal of Securities (STRIPS) are zero coupon bonds offering the option to an investor to purchase separately (not bundled) the principal or interest portions of the securities' cash flow streams. They range in denominations of $1,000 to $1 million.

113. B: State-issued general obligation (GO) bonds are backed by both income taxes and sales tax. Those issued by local governments are backed by property taxes.

114. A: Series HH bonds mature in 10 years and come in denominations of $500 to $10,000. They do pay semiannual interest (Series EE bonds do not), can only be obtained by trading in matured Series EE bonds, and cannot be purchased for cash.

115. B: Bond certificates, when issued, are not required to have the bond's state of issuance. They are required to have the call feature, paying agent, and dates of interest payments.

116. D: Book entry bonds are not evidenced by an actual physical certificate and instead have as proof of ownership the trade confirmation from the purchase transaction. Principal-only registration bonds are evidenced by an actual bond certificate printed with the owner's name. Fully registered bonds are recorded for interest and principal payments with the owner's name. Bearer bonds are issued with a bond certificate that does not have the owner's name printed on it.

117. B: A bond's yield to maturity is largely a combination of considering its annual income and the difference in price paid above, at, or below par. A bond purchased at the highest premium will produce the lowest yield to maturity, here being the bond purchased at 103. All the purchases represented here had the same coupon rates (and accordingly, the same annual income) with one purchased at 98 (a discount), 100 (at par), and two at a premium, 100 1/4 and 103. The par value received at maturity for the 103 bond will represent the largest loss to the investor of these purchases, given that he or she paid the most over par for that bond.

118. A: Given that corporate bonds are priced as a percentage of their par value of $1,000, the following calculation would provide a dollar price quote of $935 for this bond.

$$93\ 1/2\ \% = 93.50\% = 0.935$$

$$0.935 \times \$1,000 = \$935.00$$

119. B: The type of maturity represented by this example is a term maturity in that the entire issued amount of $850,000 becomes due in its entirety on one date set in advance. A balloon maturity involves the principal amount being paid over years with the largest coming due on the last date. A serial maturity bond also matures over years with the largest portions due in the later years.

120. D: Classification of options is by series, type, and class. The series classification provides that options of the same class with the same expiration month and exercise price be grouped together. There are two types of options, calls and puts. Calls provide the buyer the option to purchase a stock for a specific price and only for a specific period of time. Puts provide the buyer the option to sell a stock for a specific price and only for a specific time period. The option class provides groups according to the type of option and underlying stock.

121. C: The price of a corporate bond is determined by many different factors that include the bond's call features if any, its issuer, interest rates, and the term of the bond.

122. A: First, it's necessary to establish what this investor's breakeven price is. This is done by taking into account any money that he or she has obtained to this point as a result of this position, the per share price for selling short the shares of PTR, and the premium on the sale of the put.

$$\$42.50 + \$2 = \$44.50$$

The breakeven here is $44.50. This is the price at which this investor will neither gain nor lose on this position.

Next, in order to calculate the total maximum gain, it's necessary to take the breakeven price and subtract the share price he or she will receive as a result of the put being exercised.

$$\$44.50 - \$38 = \$6.50$$

This is the most he or she can profit, given the amounts taken in for selling shares short and receiving put premium minus the amount he or she will pay out to cover the exercised put option. The total maximum gain is: $6.50 \times 100 = \$650$

123. B: Requirements for a Uniform Gift to Minors Act (UGMA) account include that there be one minor, one custodian, and an account title stating it's a UGMA account and the state of origin for the account. Further, the assets within the account would not be registered currently in the child's name as the nominal owner but, instead, registered in the custodian's name with the child named as the beneficial owner.

124. D: Types of account ownership include partnership, trust, and joint.

125. B: The order book official actually is employed by the exchange and has the job of maintaining a fair and orderly market. An option market maker is an exchange member, a two-dollar broker is an independent member of the exchange, and a commission house broker is employed by an exchange member organization.

126. C: In a discretionary account, a registered representative cannot choose to close out an account without the client's approval, but can choose whether to buy or sell, choose the amount to buy or sell, and choose the type of asset to buy or sell.

127. D: Interest rate options can be either price based or rate based and used to profit from interest rate movements or as a hedge for Treasury securities.

128. A: The managing party of a fiduciary account may not work the account and assets in it to benefit itself, should always act according to the prudent man rule, and may have full discretion with the authority to buy and sell securities and withdraw cash and securities. They may also have a limited power of attorney giving them the authority to buy and sell securities without the ability to withdraw securities.

129. A: When opening an account for a customer, a registered representative should obtain from that customer whether he or she is an employee of a bank, citizenship status, an estimation of annual income, and a bank reference.

130. D: Examples of a fiduciary include an administrator, a guardian, and an executor.

131. B: Trust accounts can be revocable, irrevocable, complex, or simple (not basic).

132. C: LEAPS stands for Long-term Equity Anticipation Securities.

133. D: An investor looking to profit from foreign currency options would buy foreign currency calls or sell foreign currency puts, given indications that a country's stock market is experiencing levels of price increase, not decrease; indications that a country is experiencing an economic upswing, not downturn; and indications that a country is experiencing a period of government stability, not instability.

134. A: It is the principal of the firm who must take additional responsibility in monitoring these accounts over time, closely and more often than usual. A registered representative's discretionary authority is not transferable, requires a limited power of attorney that can last up to three years, and ends with the termination of his or her employment with the firm.

135. C: The Uniform Gift to Minors Act (UGMA) requires that each account have only one custodian and one minor. A custodian may oversee more than one separate account, and minors can have more than one separate account themselves. As applied to this example here, the father and mother each may be sole custodians of separate accounts for each of their three children A, B, and C.

136. B: The credited amount is a result of subtracting the call strike price paid by the investor, as they exercised their option contract, from the current index quote.

$$\$522.31 - \$509.00 = \$13.31$$

$$\$13.31 \times 100 = \$1,331$$

The net profit from this position comes from subtracting the premium he or she paid for the call from the amount credited to the account.

$$\$3 \times 100 = \$300 \text{ premium paid}$$

$$\$1,331 - \$300 = \$1,031$$

137. A: Registered representatives are not required to obtain or keep current information regarding their customers' educational statuses or backgrounds. They do need to maintain current information regarding their customers' marital statuses and investment objectives, goals, and philosophies.

138. C: Buying and selling two options at the same time of the same class but with either different exercise prices, months, or both, is called a spread. Buying a call and a put at the same time with the same stock, strike price, and expiration is called a long straddle. Selling a call and put at the same time with the same stock, strike price, and expiration is called a short straddle. Buying or selling at the same time a call and a put with the same stock and expiration but with different strike prices is called a combination.

139. D: A family limited partnership is most often utilized for personal estate planning as a vehicle for parents to transfer ownership of assets to their children and is preferred due to potential tax benefits that favor the parents versus other options.

140. B:
$$2.09 = 2 \ 9/32\% = 2.28125\%$$

$$0.0228 \times \$100,000 = \$2,280$$

The calculated premium to be paid to buy this call would be $2,280.

141. A: There is an inverse relationship between interest rates and the prices of Treasury securities. As rates move in one direction, prices move in the opposite. An investor with the opinion that rates will fall will want to utilize price-based options to profit from that movement. Rates falling signals a rise in Treasury prices. This investor will want to purchase call options to buy low in anticipation of impending higher future prices. Additionally, he or she will want to sell put options in the hopes that the option will expire without being exercised and that he or she is able to profit from the premium income received from the sale of the option.

142. C: Securities that have the brokerage firm as the registered nominal owner and the customer as the beneficial owner are considered held in street name. Transfer and ship securities and transfer and held-in-safekeeping securities are both registered in the customer's name.

143. B: A principal of the firm must accept and sign off on the new account either prior to or soon after the execution of the first trade.

144. C: The father's action as fiduciary that is outside of the fiduciary guidelines and not allowed is the naming of the child's mother with equal discretionary authority over the account. The custodian does not have the authority to transfer or share discretionary authority of the account with a third party.

145. D: Foreign currency option rules dictate that same side position limits are 600,000 contracts, not 500,000; NASDAQ options trading is 9:30 a.m. (not 9:00 a.m.) to 4:00 p.m. Eastern standard time (EST); and option expiration is on the Saturday following the third Friday, not first, at 11:59 p.m. EST.

146. C: An investor who believes shares of PPG will rise is said to be bullish for PPG. With that, they will want to purchase an option contract that will allow him or her to maximize profits. Purchasing 1 PPG August 66 call will allow him or her to make the most potential profit in the event the share price rises above its current $65 per share. The 66 call will maximize profits above the 72 call whether the stock price rises above $72 or not. Either put contract would not be appropriate, given the investor anticipates the share price rising. Any increase in PPG's share price above its current $65 will negate the investor wanting to purchase the option to sell at 52 or 64.

147. B: The breakeven takes into account the investor's original purchase price and the premium he or she was paid for selling the call. Here:

$$\$31.25 - \$1 = \$30.25$$

Selling their shares of PPG at $30.25 will allow them to neither gain nor lose on this position. A sale for any price above $30.25 will produce a gain.

The maximum gain for the position takes into account both the breakeven for the investor and the strike price for the call if exercised. Here:

$$\$38 - \$30.25 = \$7.75$$

$$\$7.75 \times 100 \text{ shares} = \$775$$

If the buyer of the call exercises his or her option to buy 100 shares of PPG at $38 per share, the seller of that call will achieve the maximum gain above the original purchase price (having taken into account the premium he or she received for selling the call).

148. D: Account statements are sent to the address noted on the customer's account. Duplicate confirmations can be sent to someone with power of attorney, but that request must be made in writing. Brokerage firms may hold a customer's account correspondence for up to two months (not one), if he or she is traveling domestically, and up to three months (not two), if he or she is traveling internationally.

149. C: An investor would not utilize index options to hedge a short portfolio by buying puts or selling calls. He or she would, however, hedge a short portfolio by buying calls or selling puts and hedge a long portfolio by buying puts or selling calls.

150. A:
$$\text{premium} = \$3 \times 100 = \$300$$

Given a strike price of 60 on this put, the interest rate is 6 percent. Rates falling to 5 percent indicate that the investor who purchased this put is in the money 10 points at expiration.
$$60 - 50 = 10 \text{ pts.}$$

Accordingly, this investor's account will be credited $1,000.

$$10 \text{ pts.} \times 100 = 1,000 = \$1,000$$

This investor paid a premium of $300 for this put option. The total profit will be as follows:

$$\$1,000 \text{ credit} - \$300 \text{ premium paid} = \$700 \text{ profit}$$

151. B: A fiduciary account requires that anyone but the beneficial owner of an account intending to enter orders for that account must provide confirmation of the authority to do so in writing.

152. C: The Options Clearing Corporation publishes a disclosure document called the Characteristics and Risks of Standardized Options, provides a guarantee as to an option's performance, and facilitates standardized options to settle on a trade date plus one. They do not, however, issue option contracts on the trade date but instead the day after the trade date.

153. A: The investor's option contract dictates that he or she paid a $200 contract premium for an option to buy 100 shares of PPG at $55 per share with the expiration of that contract being in May. The option premium must be multiplied by 100, and each contract is for one round lot of 100 shares of the contracted stock.

154. B: Uniform Gift to Minors Act (UGMA) guidelines regarding contributions include gifts being irrevocable, discretionary authority for account assets to be used for the minor's education, and a limitless gift size. Additionally, the tax-free gift limit is set at $14,000 per year, not $16,000 per year.

155. C: An option seller is the writer of the contract and his or her goal is primarily not to have the option contract exercised but instead to profit off of the premium income resulting from writing the contract itself. Further, the seller does not have the right to decline having the contract exercised. The seller, by writing the contract, does not retain rights to decline exercising the contract but assumes the role instead of having the obligation to the buyer to either sell (call) or buy (put) if the buyer of the option should choose to exercise his or her option.

156. A: A joint tenants in common (JTIC) account requires that, once deceased, that party's assets from the account become the property of the estate and do not go to the surviving party of the account. In a transfer on death (TOD) account, the parties are provided the opportunity to designate in advance who they would like their portion of the account to go to in the event they die. In a joint tenants with rights of survivorship (JTWROS) account, the death of one party of the account provides for the surviving party to retain all assets in the account. A joint account requires that all parties of the account be alive.

157. B: This position, selling a call and a put with the same stock, strike price, and expiration, is a short straddle. A long straddle is the same with the exception of being a purchase of a call and put. A combination is like a straddle except it's a purchase or sale of a call and put with same stock and expiration but different expirations. A spread is buying and selling two options at the same time of the same class but with either different exercise prices, months, or both.

158. C: In opening a corporate account, a registered representative may, if necessary, obtain a corporate charter and the corporation's bylaws that confirm his or her ability to buy securities on margin, a corporate resolution that stipulates individuals with authority to enter orders, and a certificate of incumbency stipulating the officers who can do business on behalf of the corporation.

159. A: A calendar spread consists of a long and short option with same class but different expirations:
Sell 1 PPG May 23 put
Buy 1 PPG August 23 put

A price spread consists of a long and short option with the same class but different strike prices:
Buy 1 PPG May 23 put
Sell 1 PPG May 21 put

A diagonal spread consists of a long and short option with the same class but different strike prices and expirations:
Sell 1 PPG May 21 put
Buy 1 PPG August 23 put

160. D: An investor who is long a stock ideally would like to achieve some downside price protection against loss given the possibility of the share price falling in general, and then specifically, below the original purchase price. There are two options for them doing that here.

By purchasing a put he or she is essentially purchasing the option to sell the shares of DZE at a set price that will allow profit taking, given the original purchase price. Even if the DZE share price drops, the investor will retain the option to sell the shares at the put strike price until the expiration of the contract.

By selling a call, he or she is essentially selling to another investor the option to buy the DZE shares at a set price that will allow profit taking, given the original purchase price. The investor will profit from the option being exercised by the buyer of the call due to the fact that the strike price of the call will have been set at a price above the investor's original purchase price, thereby protecting him or her from any loss in the event of a DZE share price drop. By selling the call, the investor retains the opportunity to sell the shares at a profit.

161. D: The maximum gain on this bear call spread would be the net result of the premium he or she gained on selling the call and the amount paid when buying the call.

$$\$4 - \$1 = \$3$$

$$\$3 \times 100 = \$300$$

This $300 total maximum gain will be attained if neither option is exercised and they both expire.

162. B: A bearish outlook points to the opinion that stock prices will fall. In relation to an options contract, it points to the opinion that the stock that is the subject of the contract has a future outlook of price decline. Given this, contract sellers would pursue writing call contracts so as to hopefully avoid the buyer exercising a contract to buy higher a stock whose price is in decline and profit from the premium gained by simply writing the contract. Option contract buyers would pursue purchasing put contracts so as to exercise an option to sell high a stock whose price is currently in decline. Conversely, option contract buyers would not pursue purchasing call contracts. There would be no need to purchase the option to buy high a stock in an open-end decline.

163. A: An option's premium is an extension of what its value is to the market and potential investors. The determination of the premium paid by an investor purchasing the option will be based on factors such as interest rates, supply and demand, and the timing of the option's expiration. It will not be based on the option's class and series.

164. C: Considering all of this investor's option positions, two of the four are currently in the money. These options would maximize both his or her investment and profit if exercised now.

HKP August 75 put

Shares of HKP are currently quoted at $72.50 per share. If exercised, this contract would provide the investor with the option of selling 100 shares of HKP at $75 per share when the quoted current market price is below that. To go further, the investor's profit is higher selling the shares via the option contract than selling them in the current open market.

RPT August 81 call

Shares of RPT are currently quoted at $82.75 per share. If exercised, this contract would provide the investor with the option of buying 100 shares of RPT at $81 per share when the quoted current market price is higher than that. To go further, the investor's profit is higher buying shares of RPT via the option contract than buying them in the current open market.

165. D:

$$\text{breakeven} = \text{strike price} + \text{premium}$$

$$\$78 = \$73 + \$5$$

The breakeven amount is the where the gain and loss of the transaction equalizes so as to come out no better and no worse for having participated in the transaction. Here, that amount is $78 per share.

$$\text{premium paid} = 100 \times \$5 = \$500$$

The maximum loss is the most that this investor stands to lose for having purchased this option contract. If the share price for PPG drops to below the strike price of $73 and remains there up through the contract's expiration date, the investor will not exercise the option, and the most he or she will be out is the premium paid for the contract, here $500.

The maximum gain for this investor is unlimited given that the option contract provides them with the option to buy shares at $73 per share. Every dollar of increase in share price above the breakeven price will provide a gain to the investor. With this, the potential for gain is unlimited.

166. B: This investor would have a call that is in the money given that the current stock price is greater than the option's strike price. The call provides them with the option to purchase PPG at $33 per share. With it currently trading at $36.50, he or she could exercise the option, purchase the shares at $33, and benefit from the price appreciation between the two.

167. B: With regards to transacting in a new margin account, investors are required to deposit either $2,000 in equity or half of the purchase price of the securities, whichever is greater:

Minimum equity required:
$2,000

Half of the securities' purchase price:

$$500 \times \$2 = \$1,000$$
$$\$1,000 \times 0.50 = \$500$$

In this example, the required deposit would be $1,000. The minimum equity requirement of $2,000 is greater than half of the purchase price of the securities, which is $500. Even with that, a customer's required deposit will never be more than the purchase price of the securities. Here, $2,000 is greater than the purchase price of $1,000; therefore, the purchase price of $1,000 will be the required deposit.

168. A: The statement regarding his educational background would be considered a misrepresentation and grounds for discipline. In order for it to qualify as a misrepresentation and cause for discipline, it must have been untrue and knowingly communicated to the customer. Here, this representative knowingly lied and mischaracterized his education with the intent to impress this prospective customer. The statement regarding the biotech analyst would not qualify as a misrepresentation given that, at the time, the representative made the statement that the analyst was employed by his firm. The representative cannot be held responsible for the analyst leaving even though that is largely the reason the customer signed with him and opened a brokerage account with the firm.

169. B: Government bonds are the type of investment that this representative should recommend given this investor's primary objective of generating income. Annuities and collateralized mortgage obligations (CMOs) are investments more appropriate to an investor seeking liquidity. Common stocks are more suitable for an investor with capital appreciation as his or her primary investment objective.

170. B:

$$\text{current yield} = \frac{\text{annual income}}{\text{current price (POP)}}$$

$$\text{current yield} = \frac{\$3}{\$17} = 0.1765 = 17.7\%$$

171. C: Municipal bonds would be the choice for an investor seeking investments with tax benefits. Direct participation programs and annuities are appropriate with investors primarily seeking liquidity. Corporate bonds are great for investors seeking income.

172. A: In order to provide good and complete delivery, certificates must be delivered in round lots that can be easily combined to form 100. Here, that is three certificates of 100 shares each, with one certificate for 20 shares. Six certificates of 50 shares each does not provide a complete delivery, and 30 certificates of 10 shares each with four certificates of five shares each does not qualify as good round lots.

173. D: Intangible drilling costs are 100 percent deductible for the year in which they occur and include wages, well casings, and geological surveys.

174. C: This individual should ensure that the certificate of limited partnership he or she files includes specifics regarding how to approve and incorporate new limited partners into the partnership, specifics regarding how the partnership will be dissolved, if necessary, and details of the business that the partnership will be engaging in. It will not be necessary to include the educational and professional backgrounds of all partners, limited and general.

175. D: Good delivery states that a customer must satisfy a few requirements, which include confirming that all attachments are there as well as a uniform delivery ticket included and that the signatures of all owners are present and all owners are actually living.

176. A: Regarding a new client that may qualify for institutional customer status, this representative should consider whether the client can independently determine potential investments for him- or herself and also make decisions based on his or her independent evaluations. Further, if the client meets the suitability criteria to make his or her own investment decisions, then this representative has the authority to recommend almost any investment and leave it to the client to determine whether he or she should proceed. This representative, however, should begin by ensuring that this client has at least $10 million (not $15 million) in assets in order to qualify as having institutional customer status.

177. C: This representative, in entering a market order that was influenced by information from a report that had not been made public yet, would be guilty of trading ahead. Front running involves entering a firm order before entering a customer's much larger order with the intent to profit from the market effect of that customer's large order. Capping is done with the intent to prevent the further rise of a stock price. Painting the tape is practiced by two or more individuals and involves them creating the false appearance of activity in a given security only in an effort to attract new buyers to that security.

178. A: Guidelines regarding gifts being exchanged between employees of member firms include the recipient's employer approving it first and the gift being given first to the employer to then pass along to the employee. Gifts of this type have restrictions, but are definitely not prohibited, and in fact, have a set limit of $100 or less (not $75), per person, per year.

179. B: Proxies are a type of absentee ballot provided to those shareholders who may not be able to attend shareholder meetings or vote on corporate issues in person.

180. A: Limited partners are limited in their risk to the loss of only what they've invested into the partnership. General partners handle the management of the partnership and, accordingly, may receive compensation for that management role. Additionally, general, not limited partners, have the authority to purchase property and sign off on legally binding contracts on behalf of the partnership.

181. D: An investor seeking a real estate partnership with lower risk and more predictable, steady cash flows should choose an existing property partnership. Because this would involve an existing income property, the cash flows would be very predictable, established, and immediate. With new construction, the risk is higher, and there is no guarantee of income until the property is completed, rented, or sold. With government-assisted housing, risk can be lower, but due to potential changes in government programs, cash flies may not be as predictable as this investor needs. An historic

rehabilitation partnership provides very unpredictable cash flows in that, due to being a restoration, there may be no real rental history to predict from.

182. C:

$$\text{accrued interest} = (\text{principal} \times \text{interest rate}) \times \left(\frac{\text{\# of days}}{360}\right)$$

Using a 30-day month, the number of days total = 259 days
January = 30 days
February = 30 days
March = 30 days
April = 30 days
May = 30 days
June = 30 days
July = 30 days
August = 30 days
September = 19 days
(15 days as of purchase date + 4 days for up to but not including settlement)
Saturday and Sunday are not proper settlement dates, but interest accrues on Friday (the day after purchase date), over Saturday and Sunday, and then ends Monday right up to settlement, which is Tuesday.

$$\text{accrued interest} = (\$10{,}250 \times 5.5\%) \times \left(\frac{259}{360}\right)$$
$$= (\$10{,}250 \times 0.055) \times (0.7194)$$
$$= (\$563.75) \times (0.7194)$$
$$= \$405.56$$

183. D: Churning is trading practice that is prohibited by the Financial Industry Regulatory Authority's (FINRA's) rules of fair practice and is practiced by representatives with the motive of producing higher commissions for themselves. In determining whether the practice of churning has taken place in a given account, regulators may examine whether there is a high frequency of transactions and look at the representatives' earned commissions on the accounts in question. Regulators will not, however, take into account the customer's level of profitability on the account when deciding whether churning has taken place.

184. C: The omission of an immaterial fact in relation to an investment decision by a representative to a customer would not be considered a violation of the Financial Industry Regulatory Authority's (FINRA's) rules of fair practice. The omission must be material in order for it to qualify as a violation. Violations of FINRA's rules of fair practice do include a representative making any guarantee of profit in an investment to a customer and using a pending dividend as the only reason for recommending a specific stock to a customer.

185. D: Mutual fund sales literature should utilize graphs to illustrate the fund's performance against a broad-based index, not contain general statements comparing the relative safety of mutual funds versus other investments, and note the sources for any graphs contained therein.

186. B: The Medallion Signature Guarantee Program is not free to members. They must pay a fee in order to transact through the program. The Medallion Program involves New York Stock Exchange (NYSE) members being given the authority to substitute their signatures on securities certificates

with a stamped medallion and does ensure that transfer agents accept securities transferred by member firms utilizing this program.

187. A: This investor, by seeking to invest in an oil and gas partnership with only the lowest risk, should consider an income program. This type of partnership involves existing wells that will provide not only predictable cash flows but cash flows that would begin immediately. Existing wells will always run the risk of reserves running out, but that overall risk is still low relative to other oil and gas partnership programs. An exploratory drilling program involves drilling for new reserves. Although it can provide the largest payoff, the risk is also the highest due to a low rate of success in drilling in new fields. A developmental program has less risk than an exploratory program in that the drilling is being done near proven reserves, but again, it is still risky in that the success rate for this type of drilling is relatively low.

188. D: To ensure that investment recommendations are suitable for each individual customer, representatives must review different types of customer information including their current debt loads and major expenses, their tax brackets, and their retirement plans and future needs.

189. B: This representative recommending specific technology stocks for purchase or sale to this group of investors would be considered making blanket recommendations and, accordingly, be against the Federal Industry Regulatory Authority's (FINRA's) rules of fair practice. Even though they all seem to have similar profiles as investors, there may always be some way that differentiates them and thus makes these recommendations wrong for one or more of them.

190. D: A general partner in a limited partnership has the authority to sell property on behalf of the partnership. They may not borrow funds from the partnership, engage in activities that compete directly with the partnership, or intertwine their own personal funds with those of the partnership.

191. B: A sharing arrangement that would require that all of the program costs be covered by the limited partners and only after the limited partners have made their investment back would the general partners start to receive payments is called a reversionary working interest. A disproportionate working interest has the general partner covering a small part of the costs of the partnership while receiving a significant portion of the partnership's revenue. A functional allocation involves both the limited and general partners sharing in the revenues of the partnership. An overriding royalty interest provides an individual with the opportunity to receive partnership royalties without having to take on any of the risks of the partnership.

192. C: The margin department is responsible for determining amounts owed to or by customers as well as dates related to those monies. The cashiering department processes cash and securities that are both received and distributed. The order room directs orders once received to the appropriate market to be executed and further provides confirmation once executed. The purchase and sales department interacts in the customer's account, inputting transactions and handling billing.

193. A: Due to the termination of this limited partnership, a liquidation of the partnership assets is necessary. First in line regarding order of payment upon liquidation of the partnership's assets are its secured lenders. Next in line would be its general creditors, followed by the limited partners and then the general partner.

194. D: Possible reasons for this seller's rejection of delivery could include missing attachments, providing no guarantee for signatures, physically damaged certificates, and delivering securities before the official settlement date.

195. B: This investor, in seeking a real estate partnership that will provide tax benefit as well as investment income, should avoid any partnerships involving raw land. This type of partnership provides no tax benefits or deductions to the investor. It is simply the raw land appreciation that the investor would be gaining. Government-assisted housing partnerships will provide tax credits, new construction partnerships will provide deductions on expenses and depreciation upon completion of the project, and historic rehabilitation partnerships provide tax credits and deductions.

196. C: An investor looking into investing in a limited partnership and specifically seeking an investment that produces quick income and with tax benefits attached should first analyze a partnership's time horizon and tax features. The partnership's liquidity and management abilities are also important but not first and primary to meeting this investor's objectives.

197. A: Defined benefit plans may either provide the employee with a retirement payment equal to a fixed percentage of his or her previous salary or a lifetime of fixed payments. Additionally, with this type of plan, the employer's contribution will be determined by an actuary. Because the employee's contribution will be based on factors such as life expectancy, there is no maximum of $16,500 per year.

198. C: Customer account statements must include balances, both debit and credit, and the receipt of dividends qualifies as account activity. If a customer's account goes inactive, customer account statements must be sent at least quarterly, not semiannually. Additionally, account statements must be sent only for months when the account has been active, not monthly for any year when the account has been active.

199. B: A customer in receipt of an erroneous trade report would be bound by the actual execution of the trade, not the trade as erroneously reported, assuming the trade itself was executed without error. The firm would not be bound in any way by the trade as erroneously reported.

200. C: The allowable individual retirement account (IRA) investment here is the limited partnership. Non-allowable investments include term life insurance, real estate, and margin accounts.

201. A: For bonds that pay interest semiannually, months for which interest will be paid on the 1st or the 15th include April and October, which have a span of six months between them. February and July, March and August, and April and September are only five months apart each.

202. D: With regards to educational institutions, tax-deferred accounts may be utilized by employees of schools that are state supported, such as state universities, public high schools, and state colleges.

203. B:

$$\text{accrued interest} = (\text{principal} \times \text{interest rate}) \times \left(\frac{\text{\# of days}}{360}\right)$$

Using a 30-day month, the number of days total = 47 days
January = 30 days
February = 17 days
(15 days as of purchase date + 2 days for up to but not including settlement)

$$\text{accrued interest} = (\$12,500 \times 6.5\%) \times \left(\frac{47}{360}\right)$$

$= (\$12,500 \times 0.065) \times (0.1306)$

$$= (\$812.50) \times (0.1306)$$
$$= \$106.11$$

204. C: There is no fifth business day (T + 5) settlement option. The investor may choose the buyer's option and choose the payment and delivery dates for the purchased securities; a cash settlement that settles the same day; or next-day settlement, meaning next business day.

205. A: The investment professional seeking out the department handling issues related to tender offers should make contact with the reorganization department. The cashiering department processes cash and securities that are both received and distributed. The purchase and sales department interacts in the customer's account, inputting transactions and handling billing. The order room directs orders once received to the appropriate market to be executed and further provides confirmation once executed.

206. B: The Internal Revenue Code 501C3 provides nonprofit status to organizations that include trade schools, zoos, science foundations, and parochial schools.

207. D: Transaction confirmations should include, when applicable, the settlement instructions for the transaction, a statement regarding whether the firm involved was a market maker in that security, and any specifics regarding the type of option.

208. A:

$$\text{combined account equity} =$$
$$(\text{long market value [LMV]} - \text{debit}) + (\text{credit} - \text{short market value [SMV]})$$

$$\text{combined account equity} = (\$74,000 - \$43,000) + (\$81,000 - \$57,000)$$
$$= (\$31,000) + (\$24,0000)$$
$$= \$55,000$$

209. C: A 529 plan is not a type of defined contribution plan but instead is a type of college savings plan. Profit sharing, stock bonus plans, and 401K plans are all types of defined contribution plans.

210. B: A 529 plan can be utilized as either a prepaid tuition plan for a specific school or as a college savings plan. Withdrawals can be made free of federal tax and also free of state tax in most states. Further, assets in the account remain under a donor's control up to and beyond the student reaching the age of majority.

211. D: Regarding moving a pension plan from a previous employer to a plan with a new employer, if done by rolling over the plan, more than 20 percent of the distributed amount will initially be withheld, and the employee will be required to deposit 100 percent of the plan assets into a qualified plan within 60 calendar days. If accomplished via a direct transfer, the employee will not physically possess the plan assets at any time in the process.

212. B: The Employee Retirement Income Security Act of 1974 (ERISA) provides guidelines for employee benefit plans. There are certain decisions that might be made by this employer regarding the retirement plan it provides for employees that would not be subject to ERISA's rules. These are called settlor functions and include decisions to eliminate plan options, choose plan options, and make changes to employee-level contributions. Vesting issues, however, are regulated by the ERISA guidelines.

213. C: A loan consent agreement provides authority to a brokerage firm to loan out a customer's securities. The customer, however, is not required to sign it, and securities purchased are held in the name of the brokerage firm, not in the customer's name.

214. B: There are a few different types of individual retirement accounts (IRAs), which include a simplified employee pension (SEP), educational, and traditional accounts. A margin account is not a type of IRA account.

215. A: Simplified employee pension IRAs (SEP IRAs) have a maximum for employer contributions to employees' accounts at $51,000, and the contributions employers make into their employees' SEP IRAs are tax deductible by the employer. However, in order to qualify for an SEP IRA with an employer, an employee must be at least 21 years old, not 18, and have earned at least $550 with that employer, not $1,000. Further, an employee can qualify for an employer contribution into an SEP IRA either by opening an account on their own behalf or having the employer open one for him or her.

216. C: Tax-sheltered annuities are provided to employees as retirement plans. Only employees of nonprofit or public organizations may utilize them. These include religious organizations, nonprofit hospitals, and public schools. This does not include small private businesses.

217. D: A special memorandum account (SMA) can be created by many circumstances, which include the receipt of dividends or interest into a customer's margin account or the long market value of that account increasing.

218. A:
$$\text{purchase price} = 2,000 \times \$11 = \$22,000$$

Regulation T 50%: $11,000

Customer's borrowed amount: $11,000
Customer's equity amount: $11,000

$$\text{long market value (LMV)} = \text{borrowed amount} + \text{equity}$$

$$\$22,000 = \$11,000 + \$11,000$$

- 124 -

219. C: A customer with a restricted margin account can withdraw securities from the account only by depositing cash worth 50 percent of the value of those securities. Additionally, he or she could sell securities and withdraw 50 percent (not 60 percent) or less of the proceeds from that sale or purchase marginable securities by depositing at least 50 percent (not 40 percent) of their value.

220. A: An employee who works at an unincorporated business who would like to contribute to a Keogh plan needs to have worked for that employer for at least one year. Additionally, he or she must be at least 21 years of age, not 18, and he or she needs to work at the job full time, at least 1,000 hours per year, not 750.

221. D: An investor who would like to have his or her individual retirement account (IRA) account moved to a new custodian would need to choose between having the account rolled over or transferred. Considerations should include that the frequency of a direct transfer is unlimited and that a transfer is executed by a simple signature on a transfer form. Further, he or she should be aware that a rollover can be utilized only once every 12 months.

222. A: If a customer were to sell short 1,000 shares of TXS at $11 per share and the market experienced a price decrease to $9 per share, his or her margin account would see a decrease in its short market value and a the credit balance would remain the same, not increase. Additionally, the equity would increase, not decrease.

223. C: This individual, in opening a traditional individual retirement account (IRA), will be able to contribute $5,500 to a separate account on behalf of his spouse, may be subject to both a penalty tax and income taxes if he were to make any withdrawals prior to reaching the age of 59 1/2, and will be able to contribute up to $6,500 in earned income to an account on his own behalf due to currently being over the age of 50.

224. D: A customer establishing both a long and short position that would then create a combined account would be required to meet the minimum equity for the long and short position as well as satisfy the Regulation T requirement for both the long and short positions.

225. B: Regulation T does not provide the Federal Reserve Board with the authority to oversee the frequency of credit extension to a given customer but does provide them with the authority to oversee the amount of deposit or margin required and the dates of payment for the transaction.

226. A: Regulation S-P provides that privacy notices may be sent electronically and that customers may opt out of having their nonpublic, personal information shared with third-party companies. It further requires that the firm delivers annual, not semiannual, privacy notices to its customers and that the firm delivers the first privacy notice to its customers by the time the account is opened, not within three days of the opening of the account.

227. B:

$$\text{original purchase long market value} = 250 \times \$65 = \$16{,}250$$

$$\text{original purchase Regulation T 50\% equity} = \$16{,}250 \times 0.50 = \$8{,}125$$

$$\text{original purchase borrowed amount} = \$16{,}250 - \$8{,}125 = \$8{,}125$$

When the PTR share price increased from $65 to $81, both the long market value and the customer's equity increased.

$$\text{increased long market value} = 250 \times \$81 = \$20{,}250$$

$$\text{actual increase} = \$20{,}250 - \$16{,}250 = \$4{,}000$$

$$\text{increased equity} = \$8{,}125 + \$4{,}000 = \$12{,}125$$

$$\text{increased Regulation T 50\% equity} = \$20{,}250 \times 0.50 = \$10{,}125$$

$$\text{excess equity} = \text{increased equity} - \text{increased Regulation T equity}$$

$$\text{excess equity} = \$12{,}125 - \$10{,}125 = \$2{,}000$$

228. C: A brokerage firm seeking a bank loan would like to commingle two customers' pledged securities as collateral. To do so, it is required by Securities & Exchange Commission (SEC) rule 15c2-1 to first obtain written permission from both of the customers. Further, the pledged securities of the customers may not be commingled with securities owned by the firm.

229. A: A credit agreement will not provide details of an amortization schedule in that a margin loan does not amortize. It will describe the method for interest charges, provide the terms of customer credit extension, and specify interest rates to be charged for the loan.

230. C: Securities that are exempt from Regulation T include nonconvertible corporate debt, municipal securities, U.S. government securities, and U.S. government agencies.

231. D: A brokerage customer wanting to transfer his or her account to a new firm can choose to take any assets that are not transferable through Automated Client Account Transfer (ACAT) and liquidate them, physically have them shipped, or choose to have them simply retained by the old firm.

232. C: The customer account document that, once signed, obligates a customer to provide as collateral for a margin loan the securities that were purchased on margin is called a hypothecation agreement. A credit agreement dictates the terms and conditions of the extension of credit to the customer. The reserve requirement is a required deposit banks make with the Federal Reserve Board. The customer agreement is what the customer signs upon opening an account with a brokerage firm and describes the terms of that relationship.

233. A: Regulation T of the Securities Exchange Act of 1934 provides the Federal Reserve Board the authority to control customer credit in their securities purchases as extended by brokerage firms. Regulation U regulates credit as provided by banks, Regulation G regulates credit as provided by commercial lenders, and Regulation X regulates credit as provided by foreign lenders.

234. D: Non-marginable securities include initial public offerings, options, and non-NASDAQ over-the-counter (OTC) securities. They do not include 45-day-old newly issued securities. Thirty-day-old newly issued securities, however, are considered to be nonmarginable.

235. B: A wrap account is a type of account that, for one fixed annual fee, will provide an advisory role for a customer as well as cover the account execution costs. A margin account provides a customer with the opportunity to purchase securities partially by a deposited payment and the

other portion by loan. A joint account is primarily an account whose ownership is shared by two or more adults. A numbered account is one that, as requested by the customer, is not identified by a name but instead a number or symbol.

236. D: With regards to transacting in a new margin account, investors are required to deposit either $2,000 in equity or half of the purchase price of the securities, whichever is greater.

Minimum equity required:
$2,000

Half of the securities purchase price:
$$2,500 \times \$22 = \$55,000$$
$$\$55,000 \times 0.50 = \$27,500$$

In this example, the required deposit would be $27,500. It is half of the purchase price of the securities and more than the $2,000 minimum equity required.

237. B:
$$\text{net asset value (NAV)} = \text{assets} - \text{liabilities}$$

$$\$870,000 - \$120,000 = \$750,000$$

$$\text{NAV per share} = \frac{\text{total NAV}}{\text{total \# of shares}}$$

$$\frac{\$750,000}{50,000} = \$15$$

238. C: The sales charge on an open-end mutual fund pays for items that include the commissions of representatives and their brokerage firms and the underwriter's expenses. The sales charge is not a fund expense but, instead, a cost the investor must bear that covers fund distribution. Accordingly, the sales charge would not pay for the printing of the fund prospectus or mailing expenses.

239. A:
$$\text{sales charge \%} = \frac{(\text{purchase price} - \text{net asset value})}{\text{purchase price}}$$

$$\frac{(\$8 - 7.25)}{\$8} = 0.0938 = 9.4\%$$

240. D:
$$\text{sale proceeds} - \text{original cost} = \text{capital gain per share}$$

$$\$25.75 - \$23.25 = \$2.50 \text{ capital gain per share}$$

$$3,500 \text{ shares} \times \$2.50 = \$8,750 \text{ total capital gain}$$

241. B:

$$\text{average cost per share} = \frac{\text{total amount invested}}{\text{total \# of shares}}$$

$$\frac{\$750}{37} = \$20.27$$

$$\text{average purchase price per share} = \frac{\text{total of share prices paid}}{\text{\# of purchases made}}$$

$$\frac{\$71.60}{3} = \$23.87$$

242. D: The Investment Company Act of 1940 designates three different types of investment companies: unit investment trust, management investment company, and face amount company.

243. C: An investor seeking to invest only in common stock shares has the share pricing dictated by a formula, and is provided the opportunity to receive dividends and vote, should invest in an open-end mutual fund. A unit investment trust will have a portfolio of primarily government or municipal debt, and a closed-end mutual fund would invest in common shares and debt securities as well as having share pricing determined by supply and demand.

244. A: The test established by the Investment Company Act of 1940 is called the 75–5–10 test. The asset allocations required by this test are that 75 percent of the fund's assets should come from other issuers, they should not invest in any one company more than 5 percent, and 10 percent is the maximum for owning another company's outstanding voting stock.

245. B: An investment company seeking to register with the Securities & Exchange Commission (SEC) must have at least 100 shareholders. Additionally, it must have a net worth of at least $100,000, not $150,000, and there is no requirement that states a trading minimum for the previous year.

246. D: Investment companies are not prohibited from lending money in an effort to earn interest. They are prohibited from performing the activities of a bank, trying to take control of other companies, receiving broker commissions, and operating with 100 shareholders or less.

247. C: The board of directors of a management company is not responsible for managing the portfolio of investments. They are responsible for hiring the custodian bank, monitoring the company president and others who are responsible for daily operations, and deciding the types of funds the company should offer.

248. A:

$$\text{underwriting spread} = \text{underwriting fee} + \text{selling concession} + \text{management fee}$$

$$\$1.15 + \$1.85 + \$0.65 = \$3.65 \text{ (underwriting spread)}$$

$$\text{net proceeds due to the issuer} = \text{public offering price} - \text{underwriting spread}$$

$$\$18 - \$3.65 = \$14.35 \text{ (net proceeds due to the issuer)}$$

249. C:

$$\text{annualized premium} = \frac{\text{bond premium}}{\text{\# of years left to maturity}}$$

$$\text{bond premium} = \$1{,}350 - \$1{,}000 = \$350$$

$$\frac{\$350}{5} = \$70 \text{ per year}$$

250. B: The features here that are common to both variable annuities and mutual funds are the transfer agent and custodian bank. Management for a variable annuity comes from a board of managers, and for a mutual fund, it's a board of directors. Taxation on gains and reinvestments for a variable annuity is tax deferred and, for a mutual fund, is due immediately.